Elements in Ethics
edited by
Ben Eggleston
University of Kansas
Dale E. Miller
Old Dominion University, Virginia

THE ETHICAL PHILOSOPHY OF BERNARD WILLIAMS

Alan Thomas
University of York

Shaftesbury Road, Cambridge CB2 8EA, United Kingdom

One Liberty Plaza, 20th Floor, New York, NY 10006, USA

477 Williamstown Road, Port Melbourne, VIC 3207, Australia

314–321, 3rd Floor, Plot 3, Splendor Forum, Jasola District Centre,
New Delhi – 110025, India

103 Penang Road, #05–06/07, Visioncrest Commercial, Singapore 238467

Cambridge University Press is part of Cambridge University Press & Assessment,
a department of the University of Cambridge.

We share the University's mission to contribute to society through the pursuit of
education, learning and research at the highest international levels of excellence.

www.cambridge.org
Information on this title: www.cambridge.org/9781009507219

DOI: 10.1017/9781108580953

When citing this work, please include a reference to the DOI 10.1017/9781108580953

First published 2024

A catalogue record for this publication is available from the British Library.

ISBN 978-1-009-50721-9 Hardback
ISBN 978-1-108-70642-1 Paperback
ISSN 2516-4031 (online)
ISSN 2516-4023 (print)

The Ethical Philosophy of Bernard Williams

Elements in Ethics

DOI: 10.1017/9781108580953
First published online: June 2024

Alan Thomas
University of York

Author for correspondence: Alan Thomas, ap.thomas@york.ac.uk

Abstract: This Element surveys the main claims of Bernard Williams's ethical philosophy. Topics include ethical scepticism, virtue, reasons for action, the critique of the Morality System, moral realism, and the nature of theorising in ethics.

Keywords: ethics, Bernard Williams, virtue, utilitarianism, moral realism

ISBNs: 9781009507219 (HB), 9781108706421 (PB), 9781108580953 (OC)
ISSNs: 2516-4031 (online), 2516-4023 (print)

Contents

Introduction

This Element is an introduction to the ethical philosophy of Bernard Williams (1929–2003), one of the most influential of twentieth-century British philosophers. While his contemporaries admired his brilliance, this was tempered by the view that Williams was merely a critic of the views of others.[1] Philosophers contemporaneous to Williams took themselves to be founding a new science of ethics; others constructed transcendental arguments that proved each of us must take morality to be our fundamental life project; and others developed ethical theories that claimed authority over the putative dogmatism of common-sense morality.[2]

Williams did, indeed, think that most of his peers in moral philosophy spent their professional lives building castles in the air. He thought their intellectual constructs made misplaced claims to authority over ordinary ethical experience. While critics of our ordinary experience tend to assimilate a complex range of views into a homogenous target Williams, by contrast, argued that our ordinary ethical understanding is a 'long and complex ethical tradition, with many different religious and other social strands' (Williams, 1985, p. 16).

I will emphasise that Williams's moral philosophy is more than a corrective to others' misplaced ambitions. It develops a positive ethical conception more aware of history than the neo-Sidgwickian rationalism of Williams's peers. Much of Williams's work in moral philosophy is an act of recovery. It points to aspects of our complex ordinary ethical consciousness, and recovers the ethical past, of those who inhabit a shared culture.

Two leitmotifs run throughout this Element. The first is a positive conception of 'mature' ethical agency. The second is the threat posed to it by pressure from other of our inherited ethical ideas. In Williams's terminology, this is to reject 'morality' (or 'the Morality System') from the standpoint of the 'ethical' (Williams, 1985, p. 6) and specifically to disabuse us of the idea that morality merely is the ethical in its rationally purified form.[3] This strand of interpretation examines the influence of Nietzsche on Williams's ideas and how this shapes the latter's historiography of ethics. Williams's phenomenological arguments and his historical arguments have a common task: To overcome the intellectual distortions generated by the Morality System.

Williams emphasises that this enemy is within: This system would not be as compelling were it merely an invention of philosophers. It is 'the outlook, or, incoherently, part of the outlook of almost all of us' (Williams, 1985, p. 174).

---

[1] A charge which Williams considers, and addresses, in Williams (1995k, pp. 217–219).

[2] See, for example, Parfit (1984), Nagel (1970), and Kagan (1989). In each case, Sidgwick is influential on these philosophers. For Williams's own assessment of Sidgwick's *Methods of Ethics* (1907/1962) see Williams (1995g).

[3] As this phrase is a term of art I will capitalise it throughout.

Additionally, he repeatedly identifies an asymmetric dependence of this system on our ethical ideas: The former depends on the latter, most strongly when it repudiates them.

My overall aim is to vindicate Williams's belief that while living an ethical life in our societies faces unprecedented challenges, they can be met – even if academic moral philosophy will not help us with this task. We should take seriously the implications of the title of *Ethics and the Limits of Philosophy* with its invocation of philosophy's limits. Williams's situating of this work contrasts it with 'ways in which the subject is for the most part now conducted' (Williams, 1985, p. 3). Equally, it is 'more sceptical about what the powers of philosophy are' than much of this work and, furthermore, it is 'more sceptical about morality' (Williams, 1985, p. 3).

1 The Question of Foundations

Williams presents an ideal of mature ethical agency grounded on a commitment to truthfulness and a critically reflective confidence in our form of ethical life. Why is it so hard to pin down this ideal across his writings on ethics? One reason is that his most widely read monograph, *Ethics and the Limits of Philosophy*, is, as Williams later conceded, a difficult book (Williams, 1985). It obscures his positive ethical conception. Part of the difficulty is that Williams's enquiry seems to proceed under a problematic assumption – that in ethics, as much as in epistemology, we need a foundation for our inquiries. Was this just a rhetorical strategy for what was, after all, intended as a book for the general reader – or something deeper?

1.1 Foundationalism in Epistemology and Ethics

The idea of giving a foundation to our commitments seems naturally at home in the theory of knowledge, but the idea also applies to ethics. A book that influenced Williams, Alasdair MacIntyre's *After Virtue*, exemplifies it (MacIntyre, 1981). MacIntyre argued that ethical thought was once in rational good order: It related a conception of human nature as it is to an ideal of how it might be developed. It proceeds from the former to the latter via a set of rational injunctions. (Together these constitute a 'tripartite schema'.) Then there was a 'fall' – a modernity crisis, even though the word 'modern' here picks out an event in the ancient world. For MacIntyre, every ethical thinker since that time has engaged in a forlorn, ahistorical, task of reconstructing this tripartite schema.

After Virtue argues that, in our modern condition, the failure of this project has left ordinary ethical thinking fragmented and disordered. Only one outlook avoids this predicament: the Neo-Thomist Catholicism that reflects MacIntyre's own views (MacIntyre, 2016). If you share his diagnosis, but not his outlook, then the appeal of the rationalism endemic to the Morality System becomes an obvious response to this predicament.

Williams certainly shared MacIntyre's view that any worthwhile ethical philosophy must demonstrate an awareness of the historical and social structures within which it is embedded. Did he also share his foundationalism? MacIntyre's tripartite schema is most clearly to be found in the ethical thought of Aristotle, a philosopher with whom Williams engages repeatedly – and to whom he is broadly sympathetic.[4]

In his discussion of Aristotelian ethics, we have a test case for the presence of foundationalist commitments in Williams's thinking:

> [A] person whose life fails to be the life of reason is a spoiled, imperfect, or incomplete human being. For Aristotle, ethics is based on psychology, even biology – which means in fact that *his psychology is partly ethics*. (Williams, 1993, p. 161, emphasis added).

Aristotle's search for foundations, then, must fail – we cannot get outside the ethical.[5]

Equally problematic, for Williams, is the historically important paradigm of Plato's ethics. It, too, tries to find an 'Archimedean point' for our ethical ideas; it fails for the same reason but leaves a powerful historical legacy. That legacy is a form of moral rationalism, which invokes a 'characterless' view of the self that Williams calls 'ethical Cartesianism' (Williams, 1993, p. 99). It represents a form of substractionism about the self: Even if one's self is partly composed of a purely rational self, Williams argues that one can never be merely that taken in isolation (Williams, 1985, p. 73). This false conception of the self is an important element of the Morality System.

Ethics and the Limits of Philosophy sets up its argument, at least superficially, as a search for foundations (Williams, 1985). As the book unfolds, it appears that foundationalism underpins Williams's understanding of how we are to address what he calls 'Socrates' question': 'How should one live?'. Now, Williams might well respond that the foundationalism comes not from him, but from the traditions with which he engages: the Kantian and the Aristotelian.

---

[4] On page 54 of *ELP* Williams summarises his previous chapter in a way that seems to echo the tripartite schema. He finds the 'very strong assumptions' needed to bind the elements together indefensible (Williams, 1985, p. 54). Williams's general sympathy does not extend to Aristotle's treatment of the ethical status of slaves and of women – his views receive a caustic treatment in chapter five of *S&N*.

[5] Whether this is the right question to ask about Aristotle is raised in an important interpretative essay by Martha Nussbaum (1995) to which Williams replied (Williams, 1995k, pp. 194–202).

In *ELP*'s methodological preamble, Williams justifies this assumption. He argues that there are prominent traditions in ethics that start from a minimal conception of rational agency. From that Archimedean point, these traditions develop an argument that tries to propel any agent into ethical life by the force of rational argument alone.[6] Williams diagnoses this as a political aspiration: The goal of making abstract, academic, moral philosophy itself a source of power in the world. He is unconvinced: 'What will the professor's justification do, when they break down the door, smash his spectacles, take him away?' (Williams, 1985, p. 23).

Foundationalism, I will argue, underpins Williams's arguments and is more than merely a rhetorical device for framing the issues. Specifically, it is how he addresses his recurrent concern with intellectual authority in ethics. This implicit commitment reflects MacIntyre's influence: If, as Williams believed, ordinary experience contains a reasonable pluralism of correct ethical outlooks, at what point does plurality unravel into disorder in the way MacIntyre diagnosed? A rational foundation would allow us to stabilise this structure – but what else could do so if the foundationalism fails? As we will see, Williams thought that the answer 'an ethical theory' was demonstrably unconvincing.

MacIntyre's diagnosis that ethical thought in modernity is in a state of disorder is bad news for those of us who do not share his Roman Catholic faith (MacIntyre, 2016). Williams's outlook, in contrast to MacIntyre's, is resolutely secular, liberal, and attuned to the inherent reflectiveness of an ethical life lived under the special conditions of a modern society. Does anything survive to sustain the hopes of that which – in a revealing epigraph to *ELP* – Williams characterises as the perspective of the 'chastened realist'? (The phrase is taken from a poem by Wallace Stevens.) From amidst the ruins, as it were, positive commitments do survive. That is because, Williams argued, we see them for the first time when they have been freed of distortions imposed on them by both the Morality System and its intellectual shadow, the mainstream of academic moral philosophy.

What are these commitments? In a crucial passage of *ELP*, Williams contrasts the search for 'social and political honesty', as Enlightenment ideals, with a much more ambitious conception of them foisted on us by 'a rationalistic metaphysics of morality' (Williams, 1993, p. 159). The core Enlightenment value, Williams claims, is *critique* – 'the spirit of political and social truthfulness' (Williams, 2002, p. 4).

Williams viewed this task of critique as identifying, articulating, and metaphorically 'placing' our ethical commitments in relation to other conceptions of objectivity. This is pursued via Williams's historical writing and his late

---

[6] See also 'the Amoralist' in Williams (1972).

commitment to the method of genealogy. The most important act of 'placing' is to understand our ethical ideas in relation to another important expression of our rational nature, namely, scientific understanding. There is no detaching Williams's conception of the objectivity of the ethical from his conception of what he called 'the scientific' (Moore, 2007). Modern science has given us a glimpse of a conception of a world maximally – but not totally – independent of our distinctive particularities as knowers (Thomas, 2006, chapter six).

While it makes sense to understand the scientific as a way of finding our way around a unitary physical world, the ethical, for Williams, is a way of structuring a plurality of ways of living internal to the ethical. But within each of those ways of life, there is something to which one can appeal: An ideal of mature ethical agency that is shaped by the agent's acknowledgement of the demands of the social. Those demands are reflected in an internalised 'other' who is a person one can respect. It would be shameful not to live up to the standards shared with this internalized figure (Williams, 1993, p. 98).

In Section 4, I discuss whether Williams's contrast between the absolute conception of the world implicit in our scientific understanding of it is intended to contrast with the pluralism internal to our ethical lives – to problematize the latter. In fact, Williams did not believe this was the most interesting way in which one could be a sceptic about ethics (Williams, 2016). If modern ethical scepticism characteristically takes the form of asking how moral values 'fit in' to a modern, disenchanted, scientific worldview, Williams is more interested in a local form of scepticism *within* the ethical. He thinks that we ought to focus our scepticism on the Morality System.

Given his scholarly interest in Plato, Williams identifies the origin of this System in Plato's rationalism (Williams, 1998). This rationalism finds canonical modern expression in the work of Kant (via the ancient Stoics) and has a strong presence in the recent development of ethical theories. Strikingly, Williams traces all these expressions of rationalism to a set of nine commitments.

They are as follows: The Morality System is focused on practicality, in the sense that one's obligations must always be something the agent can do (Williams, 1985, p. 175); such obligations cannot ultimately conflict (Williams, 1985, p. 176); all specific obligations are grounded on general obligations (Williams, 1985, p. 175, pp. 185–186); moral obligations are 'inescapable' – an agent is always within the scope of blame (Williams, 1985, p. 177); obligations can be trumped only by other obligations (Williams, 1985, p. 180); all important ethical considerations are translatable into obligations (Williams, 1985, p. 179); moral luck is impossible because of the purity of morality (Williams, 1985, pp. 195–196); the characteristic reaction of the system is blame, always 'directed to the voluntary' (Williams, 1985, pp. 177–178); morality is essentially impersonal in the negative sense that 'the thought *I did it* has no special significance' (Williams, 1985, p. 177).

Revealingly, when Williams states that he takes the primary exposition of the system to be the moral philosophy of Kant, he adds that 'the purity of morality itself represents a value . . . . the ideal that human existence can ultimately be just' (ibid., p. 195) Williams interprets this as Kant's secularised version of the Pelagian heresy 'which ... adjust[s] salvation to merit' (Williams, 1985, p. 38, p. 224, fn. 20). The Pelagian heresy, propounded by Pelagius (c355–c420 AD) and condemned by the Catholic Church, denies original sin, believes in the fundamental goodness of humanity, and sets humanity the task of freely achieving an ethical life without the need for God's grace.

Williams believed that if we can free ourselves from the snares of the Morality System, we achieve a conception of the ethical as reasonably pluralist, historically informed, genealogically vindicated in its core commitments and centred on an ideal of mature ethical agency. It is this positive conception that I will now exposit in more detail.

1.2 The Ethically Mature Agent

Williams's basic thesis is that a mature ethical agent has a fully developed (but not 'perfected') character. Once an agent has a mature ethical identity, then he or she acts *from* it in a way that expresses their practical identity. Practical identities are constituted by fundamental ground projects: 'Some project or objective with which the agent is deeply identified' (Williams, 1995a, p. 5).

There is a tight circle of interconnected ideas here, but the most fundamental is that of character. It allows us to explain further concepts important to Williams such as practical necessity, an agent's (in)capacities, and what it is to act from integrity. If we must use the classificatory terminology of academic writing about ethics, then Williams is primarily a virtue ethicist.

The fundamental idea is that, as Elizabeth Anscombe originally claimed, virtues of character are central to any defensible moral psychology (Anscombe, 1958). Williams concurred that the concept 'has to be used in moral philosophy' (Williams, 1985, p. 9). A virtue is 'a disposition of character to choose or reject actions because they are of a certain ethically relevant kind' (Williams, 1985, p. 9).

One of Williams's most insightful remarks about the virtues figures obliquely in his critique of 'two level' forms of utilitarianism:

> The dispositions help to form the character of an agent who has them, and they will do the job the theory has given them only if the agent does not see his character purely instrumentally, but *sees the world from the point of view of that character*. (Williams, 1985, pp. 107–108, emphasis added)

One's character is, as it were, fixed by triangulation: It emerges from coordination with two other points (Thomas, 2005, 2010, 2024). First, you identify that *on which* it is a point of view, namely, the values to which it is a response via 'feeling and judgement'. Second, it is characteristic of the virtue terms that typically are ascribed from an interpreter's point of view. It is a community that shares the understanding of that concept which, for example, judges a person to be kindly in her dealing with others.

This account of ethical judgment is essentially complemented by Williams's explanation of whether it is a form of heteronomous motivation (in Kant's sense) to act merely in this third personal light of how others see you. Williams argues not: In his positive conception, the correlate of the third person is an internalized other with a distinctive characterisation:

> [A]n internalised other [that] still has some independent identity . . . . not just a screen for one's own ethical ideas but . . . . the locus of some genuine social expectations. (Williams, 1993, p. 98)

Specifically, this 'other' represents a person whom one respects such that it would be shameful not to live up to their expectations (Williams, 1993, p. 98).

Triangulation from values, and any given community of interpretation, allows us to identify the ethical self who 'sees the world from the point of view of that character'. But, as Mark Sacks puts it, this self is always 'behind the lens' (Sacks, 2005). This looks like a conception of virtue as a form of knowledge which, to a point, it is – Williams's 'non-objectivism' about the ethical which I will discuss in Section 4 explains why the qualifier is apposite.

There is a similarity between Williams's views and those of French existentialist Jean-Paul Sartre (Sartre, 1956; Thomas, 2010, 2024). They agree on the systematic elusiveness of the self (Sacks, 2005). Both also think that there is an implicit hierarchy to our practical commitments structured via fundamental ground projects (Thomas, 2010). At the apex of this hierarchy are the most important ethical identities. An agent is identified with them; they are the perspective *from which* she acts. Williams adds that they answer the question of why one goes on at all (Williams, 1981b, p. 13). It is the idea of acting from your own ethical identity which explains Williams's use of the term 'expressive': A virtuous agent's actions are expressive of their character.

If ethics is a way of navigating a social world, we must presuppose that in characterising this agent we are talking about someone who inhabits our world – where 'our' is always a problematic expression in Williams given his attentiveness to social and political context. Our envisaged agent lives in modern liberal society which has a certain conception of law (Williams, 1993, pp. 65–68). That conception extends, importantly, beyond the idea of penalising crimes to the broader idea of civil wrongs ('torts'). Indeed, it extends to the very idea of a self who enters into the kinds of commercial contracts that constitute many of our impersonal relations to others (Thomas, 2019). In particular, generalised social trust requires the stability of the self (Williams, 2002, pp. 200–202). This matters, because our envisaged subject is embedded in a social context that negotiates ways in which the ideas of the voluntary and the responsible are related. In so doing, it identifies one way of legally ordering social life – not *the* way. The Morality System implies that there is only one such correct ordering – one which assumes a metaphysically ambitious notion of the voluntariness of action.

If this agent is reflective and historically informed, they may have the thought that the ways in which these basic concepts of freedom, law, voluntariness, and ethical reactions relate to each other can be found in some canonical texts of the Western cultural tradition. They can find this out via reflection on ordinary ethical practice and its persistent defiance of the tenets of the Morality System. In *S&N*, Williams argues that the apparently 'archaic' emotion of shame still does a lot of ethical work for us – for example, in his model of the internalized other (Williams, 1993). That is a truth of our experience: *S&N* does not teach it to our envisaged agent but reminds her that she uses this concept already to make sense of her ethical experience.

Assembling the pieces, then: The basic idea for making sense of our ethical lives is that of virtue. This is a multitrack character disposition that goes beyond a mere skill because it involves characteristic patterns of motivation (Williams, 1985, p. 9). Specific practical questions focus a person's virtues on a course of action. From the third personal perspective, one of the most interesting aspects of this is that a person can manifest character via the category of the unthinkable – what it does not even occur to that person to do (Williams, 1973b, p. 93; 1981f, p. 129). Furthermore, specific practical questions focus on a range of virtues in a way that can be surprising to the deliberating agent, can create new forms of (fallible) self-knowledge, and give substance to that which Williams calls moral incapacities (Williams, 1995d). The latter explains those things an agent cannot *knowingly* do.

Williams believed that there was ethical significance to agency because the ethically mature agent knows that she will be held answerable for what she does – not simply what she does voluntarily. We have a workable idea of the voluntary: It is no more than a mature ethical agent deliberating and acting from a normal state of mind (Williams, 1995b). As in other cases we may have only an implicit grasp of normalcy here, but we have an explicit grasp of non-normal conditions on deliberation and action (Thomas, 2011, p. 158).

If Williams is right, this characterisation of an ethical agent ought to strike us as truistic. It will draw us back to facts evident either from our experience or from those of others known to us through testimony. It is the removal of theoretical distortions of our ethical experience imposed by philosophical assumptions embedded in the Morality System.

Yet it is important not to forget that 'ethical Cartesianism' is one strand of the historical traditions that inform common-sense morality. It is not as if there is nothing in our ordinary conceptions to which these theoretical reflections can appeal. Furthermore, as we begin to explore Williams's approach to issues such as moral luck, we are likely to feel ourselves torn in our allegiances. This reinforces Williams's argument that the Morality System is reflected in what we already think: Giving up these ideas imposes costs on us. The controversy that Williams's views have occasioned offers ample evidence of his point – as I will illustrate in the next section.

2 Impartiality and the De-centring of Character

As each of us navigates our lives, it is a truism that we do so *from here* in the light of our characters shaped by our life experiences. However, if we start to raise reflective questions about the conduct of our lives do we possess the capacity to take a step back – to become reflectively detached? Furthermore, could this capacity for reflection be a way of thinking more objectively about what we ought to do (Nagel, 1986)?

The ideal of objectivity invoked when this question is answered positively can be more or less ambitious. More ambitiously, it demands a de-centred view of the ethical world from which our specific identity is wholly 'bleached out' – as is everyone else's. We adopt the conception of the world held by Hare's idealised agent in his 'World Agent Model': This agent takes an impartial view of everyone's practical concerns, aggregated, and acts on that basis (Hare, 1981; Williams, 1985, pp. 83–84, 87–88; Williams, 1988, p. 186). R.M. ('Dick') Hare was one of the twentieth century's most influential moral philosophers whose work Williams often takes as his target of critique; they had a personal connection – Hare was one of Williams's undergraduate tutors.

Less ambitiously, the impartial perspective informs decisions that are irreducibly personal: We combine truths from the impartial perspective with the reasons disclosed to us from the personal, engaged, perspective of our individual agency (Nagel, 1986). If Hare's model is merely a heuristic, by contrast, Nagel's view expresses his theory of the person. We are essentially composite selves where one part of us fits Williams's description of the reduced self of 'ethical Cartesianism' (Nagel, 1991).

In critiquing these different ways of framing the demands of impartiality Williams asks a question that runs deeper than his account of character, namely, is there such a thing as the practical use of reason? Williams thinks that there is. It can be demarcated in this way: Theoretical reasoning can take a first personal form, but never essentially; practical reasoning, by contrast, is essentially first personal (Williams, 1985, pp. 67–69). Williams thereby defends an intrinsic connection between the engaged standpoint of practice and the first person.

2.1 The Importance of the First Person

A continual interlocutor with Nagel, Williams's critique of impartialism seems closely to track Nagel's different formulations of that ideal. Essential first personality appears in *ELP* immediately after Williams's critique of Kant's failed attempt to ground ethics in an impartial perspective:

> [W]hat we are looking for is an argument that will travel far enough into Kant's territory to bring back the essential conclusion that a rational agent's most basic interests must coincide with those given in a conception of himself as a citizen legislator of a notional republic; but does not bring back the more extravagant metaphysical luggage of the noumenal self. (Williams, 1985, p. 65)

What notion of impartiality could help the contemporary impartialist to conduct a salvage operation from this Kantian wreckage?

The first step would be to note that a rational agent does not merely act from reasons but '*on* reasons' (ibid). Call this the fact of cognitive autonomy. Williams asks whether that is enough to bring in an impartial perspective on one's first-order beliefs and desires such as to generate a standpoint from which they can be assessed:

> If he acts *on* reasons, then he must not only be an agent but reflect on himself as an agent, and this involves him seeing himself as one agent among others. . . . he stands back from his own desires and interests, and sees them from a standpoint that is not that *of* his desires and interests. (Williams, 1985, pp. 65–66)

If we can motivate this step, then we do seem able to generate what the neo-Kantian needs: Individual agents will become legislators for all other agents (Williams, 1985, p. 66).

But Williams is sceptical. He begins his critique by pointing out that Kantian cognitive autonomy cuts across the theoretical and the practical uses of reason: That is a problem for the impartialist *about ethics*. Rational freedom involves 'standing back' from both beliefs and desires; in the latter case, reflection itself may generate new desires. Williams concedes that this may well be an insight into theoretical reasoning but, for that reason, it helps to identify an asymmetry between theoretical and practical reasoning. This asymmetry undermines the impartialist project of reconstruction:

> [P]ractical reasoning is first-personal, radically so, and involves an I that must
> be more intimately the I of my desires than this account allows. (Williams,
> 1985, p. 67) [7]

Theoretical reflections about the word are essentially world directed which explains why 'I occur in them, so to speak, only in the role of one who has this thought' (Williams, 1985, p. 67). By contrast, practical reflection isolates the essential first personality of practical thinking:

> The action I decide on will be mine and . . . . its being mine means not just that it
> will be arrived at by this deliberation, but that it will involve changes in the world
> of which I shall be empirically the cause, and of which these desires and this
> deliberation itself will be, in some part, the cause. (Williams, 1985, pp. 68–69)

Stepping back in thought, as an expression of rational freedom, does not commit the agent to take the results of other people's similar reflections as a datum to be accommodated. Nor, crucially, does it introduce the aim of the 'harmony of everyone's deliberations' – the agent is not forced to become a legislator for others.

Those parallel thoughts *do* apply to theoretical reflection. But there is a deeper explanation of why this should be so. The constitutive aim of theoretical reflection is truth – and that is not simply because it is a form of reflection (Williams, 1985, p. 69). I should take seriously the perspective of those rational agents who also want the theoretical truth, because it is a constraint on our practice of finding things out that we are all investigating a unitary physical world (Thomas, 2006, p. 93; Moore, 2007). The basis of the asymmetry between theoretical and practical reasoning is that because belief constitutively aims at truth, theoretical reflection about beliefs has the same interest merely at one remove – truth. In the case of desire, practical reflection on our conduct need not share the same constitutive aim as the desires expressed by it.

If we mistakenly construe reflection as detachment, as the impartialist does, then Williams claims that the disengaged self would have no reason at all to see any of its desires as objects to be satisfied. They become, as it were, *merely* data (a point that will prove to be important in Section 5). From the first order, engaged, perspective, I act from my desires; if reflection on them is to detach from them, then there is a radical break between reflection and agency.

The target here is clearly Nagel, whose commitment to the intellectual authority of the impartial point of view evolves, but is never abandoned (Nagel, 1970, 1986). This is, I think, clear from what Williams goes on to say next. Suppose reflection forces the practically rational agent to become a legislator: He or she has to accommodate the symmetrical perspective of all other agents and seek

---

[7] For a fascinating defence of Williams's thesis on independent grounds see Stroud (2011).

a harmony of practical interests. What is left, Williams asks, of the permission to live one's own life (Williams, 1985, p. 70)? One response is that we are allowed to put those permissions 'back in'. However, that seems to Williams a bad answer to a bad question. The idea that the individual needs permission to re-insert a concern with her organising ground projects shows that our enquiry has already gone awry.

His challenge to the impartialist is this: If the underlying moral psychology is that of 'ethical Cartesianism', as Williams puts it, 'does it leave anyone in particular for me to be?' (Williams, 1985, p. 70). In the Procrustean bed of the impartialist, one's concerns are either fully altruistic or fully egoistic with no space in-between for, for example, Williams's ground projects interpreted as 'personal commitments that are not necessarily egoistic but are narrower that those imposed by a universal concern or respect for rights' (Williams, 1985, p. 70).

2.2 Cognitive Autonomy and 'Internal' Reasons Ascriptions

There are often multiple routes to the same conclusion in Williams's work. The critique of impartialism set out in *ELP* is a culmination of arguments dating back to 'Internal and External Reasons' (Williams, 1981e). Williams there argued that all ascriptions of reasons to an agent must bear what he called an 'internal' interpretation. The basic idea is that given that reasons are fundamentally both normative and explanatory, then any reason ascribed to an agent must potentially explain some action of hers in a distinctive way (Williams, 1981e, 1995c; Thomas, 2006, chapter 4; Finlay, 2009).

Add to this Williams's further thesis that the fundamentality of ground projects implies that all the reasons potentially available to an agent who deliberates soundly are dependent on their deliberative starting point. Combine those claims and we must forgo a particular guarantee integral to the Morality System. That guarantee is that moral reasons must form part of every agent's reasons – in the expanded sense of that word which Williams calls the agent's 'subjective motivational set'.

For the rationalist, altruistic reasons are already in every agent's subjective motivational set or sound deliberation can put them there. No matter what your starting point, then, it is an a priori truth that morality is everyone's ground project. Ascriptions of reasons for action to an agent must explain specifically why that agent acts for that reason and, in so doing, explain why they saw that action in a favourable light (Williams, 1981e). We want to contrast correct deliberation with cases of error or action from ignorance. However, 'good' cases where reasons both justify and explain an action need share no interesting similarities with the failed cases (Hornsby, 2008). Williams thinks that it is an a priori truism that correct reasons ascriptions also explain why an agent acted as she did (Thomas, 2002, p. 137). This paper also foreshadows Williams's later concerns given the way in which this comparatively early, and very abstract, discussion of reasons connects to his later critique of the Morality System.

If there is a characteristic Williams's word it is 'bluff'. 'Internal Reasons' gives the example of Owen Wingrave, the eponymous hero of Benjamin Britten's opera, who is from a military family. The family insist that Owen has a reason to continue its traditions and join the army. He is equally convinced that he does not. Williams comments that Owen's family are 'bluffing' in a particular way; the family's charge against Owen is that he is *irrational* (Williams, 1981e, p. 110).

I think Williams's paper is best interpreted as a rejoinder to Nagel's influential book *The Possibility of Altruism* (Nagel, 1970). Nagel argued that the method of transcendental argument can show that every practically rational agent has an a priori interest in acting altruistically.[8] For it to be possible for one person to act directly to promote the interests of any other (the 'altruism' of his title), the former must have a conception of herself as one person extended through time, and as one person amongst other people equally real.

This is not the place to dissect the internal complexities of Nagel's argument (Thomas, 2009, chapter four). But its key features are these: Its commitment to the method of transcendental argument; the ambition of the conclusions it draws (a priori) from the very concept of a practically rational agent; and its defence of the overriding rational authority of moral reasons. They are, as Nagel memorably puts it, reasons from which one cannot 'beg off' (Nagel, 1970, p. 4).

The Wingraves think that Owen has a moral reason from which he cannot 'beg off'. It is not merely a good reason for Owen: His family argue that it is one of Owen's reasons 'already' (without the temporal implication). That makes sense if Nagel is right – If moral reasons are inescapably present in everyone's subjective motivational set. Furthermore, and this is the point that interests Williams, were Nagel correct then the Wingrave family could substantiate their charge of irrationality against Owen.

Williams inverts this argument: Your starting point in deliberation determines where sound practical deliberation can take you. So, there is no guarantee of convergence on moral reasons as a presupposition of everyone's ground project. From Williams's perspective, Nagel's neo-Kantian style of argument creates a gap between two ideas: that of *reasons for an agent* and *an agent's reasons*. Ironically, at this point, Williams claims that Kant is on his side in this

---

[8] Transcendental arguments take a 'how is this so much as possible' form: They assume some fact and ask what (a priori) conditions make it possible. They aim to establish a conclusion that is both universal and necessary. Nagel extended this strategy from reasons of belief to reasons of action.

argument: The latter reciprocally stipulates an account of practically rational agency and an account of reasons for an agent such that the two ideas – *reasons for an agent* and *an agent's reasons* – cannot possibly come apart (Williams, 1995k, p. 220, fn. 3). For Williams the question is: Why accept Kant's stipulation?

I have already noted the deeper background issue: the fate of psychologism. Nagel maintains that the science of psychology can, in part, be conducted a priori: Human psychology must be aligned with an order of reasons (Nagel, 1997). By contrast, Williams thinks that the psychology of human action is not trying to align itself with a metaphysics of reasons. That is why, for Williams, the direction of explanation runs from an agent's reasons to the idea of reasons for an agent.

On some issues Williams and Nagel share common ground; on others they are far apart. The basic picture of action in *The Possibility of Altruism* is Aristotelian: The idea of an action explanation that did not mention a 'desire state' is, for Nagel, absurd. The distinction he wants to draw is between chains of practical reasoning that begin from a desire, and others that begin from the acceptance of the truth of a proposition that, in turn, motivates both an action and the desire to perform that action. This distinction between unmotivated and motivated desires is one of the linchpins of the book and Williams (as a fellow Aristotelian on this point) has no disagreement with it.

However, this threatens to make Williams's critique of external reasons become elusive. If, by coming to believe that she has a reason, an agent can thereby acquire that which Nagel calls a 'consequentially ascribed' motive – then does not that claim automatically make all reasons ascriptions 'internal' in Williams's sense? If a person lacks a desire, then by coming to accept a truth, she acquires one anyway and hence also the reasons that this desire makes available.

This point helps to identify Williams's challenge: What is it to *come to accept* the truth of a proposition about action in the first place (Williams, 1981e, p. 108)? For Nagel, you write the theory of reasons for an agent first, and then the theory of an agent's reasons follows from it: That is the form taken by his radical anti-psychologism. For Williams, the direction of explanation is reversed: We begin from the idea of an agent's subjective motivational set and enrich its contents by sound practical deliberation (including our use of the imagination). We have no a priori guarantee that all agents will converge on what Nagel presents as the truth of basic moral principles guaranteed to be in everyone's subjective motivational set.

This focus on an agent's capacities follows from Williams's thesis that all reason statements true of an agent must be potentially explanatory of that which an agent may come to do after sound deliberation (Thomas, 2006, chapter four; Finlay, 2009). The deeper issue is Kant's democratisation of morality such that the requirements that moral truths place on agents' psychological capacities are undemanding. A psychologically realistic account of agency shows us, in Williams's view, that Kant's optimism about the universal accessibility of moral motivation is false (Skorupski, 2007). Williams's argument is a normative one, grounded on a view of sound practical deliberation. An apparently abstruse discussion of the nature of reasons leads directly, in his view, to a diagnosis of the Morality System's errors in its treatment of blame.

2.3 Morality and the Social Function of Blame

Williams argues that the Morality System is unhelpfully obsessed with blame. For him, it is just one ethical reaction we can have towards others amongst many possible reactions, one where we acquire our understanding of what it is to be blamed via the experience of being unjustly blamed (Williams, 1995a, p. 16):

> Blame rests, in part, on a fiction; the idea that ethical reasons, in particular the special kind of ethical reasons that are obligations, must, really, be available to the blamed agent. *He ought to have done it*, as moral blame uses that phrase, implies *there was a reason for him to do it*, and this certainly intends more than the thought that we had reason to want him to do it. It hopes to say, rather, that he had a reason to do it. But this may well be untrue: it was not in fact a reason for him, or at least not enough of a reason. (Williams, 1995a, p. 16 [italic in the original])

The Wingrave family blamed Owen for being irrationally at fault – for not having a reason he ought to have. But, according to the internal reasons thesis, Owen had no such reason; his family were bluffing. He was being confronted by a socially sustained fiction: His family are attempting to 'recruit' him into 'their' deliberative community:

> Under this fiction, a continuous attempt is made to recruit people into a deliberative community that shares ethical reasons, and the truth misperceived by the reconciler's causal story is this, that by means of this fiction people may indeed be recruited into the community or kept within it. (Williams, ibid.)

This 'proleptic' theory of blame, as Williams calls it, invokes the contrast between the first person and the social point of view (Williams, 1995c).[9] If this institutionalised practice of blame is regarded merely as a 'device' – wholly third personally – we would be alienated from it as merely a form of social control. But it appeals to our reasons in just the way that Kant thought that we must in order to cultivate our characters as effective instruments of the moral law. The proleptic theory appeals to 'the desire to be respected by people whom, in turn, one

---

[9] 'Prolepsis' means 'the representation of an existent before it comes into existence'.

respects' (Williams, 1995c, p. 41). This mechanism works, then, only if we have other ethical dispositions and motivations beyond blame as the Morality System understands it.

Given that there literally cannot be any external reasons in Williams's sense, in our actual practice we must be witnessing the deployment of what he called 'optimistic' internal reasons statements with this feature: They seek to make it true that people 'have' the reasons that we take as the ground for blaming them (Williams, 1981, p. 111; Williams, 1995c, p. 40; Thomas, 2015, p. 254). The proleptic theory describes how this mechanism operates: A person who lacks an appropriate reason to be blamed in a 'focused' way nevertheless has this other desire-cum-disposition, which invokes respect. Blaming triggers the mechanism such that the agent has now made it true that she has reason to avoid the action that would lead those others (whom she respects) to blame her. If this mechanism succeeds, the recruit sees the process of conversion as the acquisition of a new set of reasons:

> But the fact that blame tries to work in this way is doubtless connected with the fiction of the agent's having reason to act in the required way, and with the fact that the stance of the scrupulous blamer is that of a transferred or identifying deliberator, a fellow member of the community of reason. These features lead blame, too, towards an ideal of the absolutely voluntary act. (Williams, 1995a, p. 16)

This appeal to a proleptic mechanism, importantly, does not restore Kantian universalism about blame; it is a contingent question of whether people have this 'ethically important disposition' or not (Williams, 1995c, p. 41; Thomas, 2015, p. 254). Thus, Kant is once again key to this discussion: He thinks we directly experience 'a conclusion of practical necessity' in which motivation is given by reason alone that need not involve any desire (Williams, 1995a, p. 17). Hence, for Kant, true freedom is action done from duty – the guise in which the moral law presents itself to beings with our finite nature.

Williams certainly does not deny the existence of an agent's particular experience of acting from practical necessity. His disagreement is with Kant's explanation of it:

> [T]hey are determined by projects that are essential to the agent. In well socialized agents, many of these projects will be compatible with, indeed expressive of, ethical considerations, and we can understand why that should be so. But not all or everyone's are, and it may not be at all clear which are, and which are not, and how. One form of moral luck lies in never having to find out. (Williams, 1995a, p. 17)

Kant's claims about necessity ground his claims about universality, and it is the latter that is the focus of Williams's doubts.

As Williams notes in his account of the Morality System's attempt to make morality luck free that aspiration appears in ancient Stoicism. But the Stoics never doubted that it was a matter of constitutive luck whether or not one could be a moral agent in the first place. For Kant, that deeper issue of luck must be resolved such that morality is luck free 'all the way down'. Yet this must also be true of people for whom it cannot also be a matter of luck that they have the capacities to respond to those demands at all. The next section continues Williams's diagnosis of how, in the hands of the rationalist impartialist, the attempt to 'purify' morality distorts both the ideas of immunity from luck and the nature of voluntary action.

3 Morality, Voluntariness, and Luck

People have various desires, concerns, and practical projects. Williams conceives of them as hierarchically structured: At the top are those structuring identifications which organise lower order commitments (Thomas, 2009). These identifications can be drawn from a common stock of social scripts (Larmore, 2010). The elusive ideal of authenticity need not take the form of radically experimenting with new ways of life; you can make a standard identification your own. People may identify with being creative artists, or homemakers; not novel identifications, but the kinds of ways people want to be thought of and acknowledged by others (Thomas, 2015, 2019). Might one's adoption of any such ground project clash with the impartialist's claim that morality is supposed to be everyone's ground project? I broached some of Williams's doubts about the claim in the previous section. I turn now to how this tension manifests itself in decisions of such importance that we could call them 'existential'.

3.1 Existential Decision and the Grounds of Morality

Suppose you are a wealthy person – a successful trader, for example. But it is not how you see yourself; you see yourself as a creative artist. However, you also chafe within what seems to you a competitive and claustrophobic artworld. You both desperately want peer approval but think that your art will flourish only away from those people – (provided enough people in your destination speak French). This is a thumbnail sketch of the nineteenth-century French artist Paul Gaugin. [10] He is the subject of Williams's famous example of an individual faced with a life-defining choice between a structuring identity and the demands of morality (Williams, 1981c).

---

[10]　The case Williams discusses is not the actual Gauguin, rather, he has the features of a literary character who – confusingly – was modelled on Gauguin. (In Somerset Maugham's novel *The Moon and Sixpence.)*

This example was Williams's vehicle for exploring the tension between the importance of ground projects and the Morality System's aspiration to make morality luck free. Williams thinks that, to buy plausibility, the thesis that morality is immune to luck must narrow its scope. Paradigmatically, Kant restricts it to the thesis that the luck-free part of morality is 'unconditioned' moral value: When it comes to character, all that counts is motive; and when it comes to action, all that counts is intention (Williams, 1981c, pp. 20–21). There is one element of constitutive luck that the ancient antecedents of the view included, but which Kant excluded, namely, that there is no luck in being able to be a moral agent at all. In that sense, as Williams notes, the Kantian refinement of the ancient view develops it into a view of the world as fundamentally just: Pelagianism, once more.

One reason why the Morality System is deeply appealing is that if your aim is to make your life immune from bad luck, and morality is exempt from luck, then you have a strong motivation to live a moral life (Williams, 1981c, p. 21):

> [T]here is a kind of value which is, unlike others, accessible to all rational agents .... it must have a claim on one's most fundamental concerns as a rational agent, and in one's recognition of that one is supposed to grasp, not only morality's immunity to luck, but one's own partial immunity to luck through morality. (Williams, 1981c, p. 21)

There is a tension between the Nagelian claim that moral reasons are already in everyone's motivations and the view that morality offers an inducement to agents to embrace it and *thereby* liberate themselves from luck. We are all so Kantian that the phrase 'moral luck' does indeed sound like an oxymoron, but that is puzzling given that, as Williams also puts it, the goal of making morality luck free 'is bound to be disappointed' (ibid).

The distinction between the ethical, broadly conceived, and the Morality System narrowly conceived makes Williams's thesis about this inevitable disappointment expressible: Ethics, in the broad sense, is more honest about its relationship to luck than the Morality System (Williams, 1995j, p. 241). Furthermore, we can find this honesty in our own tradition because Aristotle's ethics exemplifies it (ibid, p. 241).

For Williams, it is a 'bitter truth' that ethics is subject to constitutive luck (ibid). However, that is not his primary concern when he discusses moral luck: His focus is Kant's view of how immunity from luck impacts an agent's understanding of her own actions. Kant guarantees that 'at the ultimate and most important level, it cannot be a matter of luck' whether a person was justified in acting in the way she did (ibid). Why does Williams think that this guarantee is unavailable? The several examples in Williams's 'Moral Luck' paper constitute his explanation. He begins with a prior question: For which human activities do we have reason to be grateful even when their exercise imposes costs on others?

> As Nietzsche constantly reminds us, morality owes a great deal, including its own existence, to the fact that it is not obeyed; it can seem to achieve closure on its own absolute kind of value only because the space in which it operates is created, historically, socially, and psychologically, by the kind of impulse that it rejects. (Williams, 1995j, p. 245)

This is a characteristic diagnosis: The asymmetric dependence of commitments of the Morality System on a broader conception of the ethical on which they depend, but can only, in its own terms, repudiate. The Morality System, far from being a rational purification of the ethical (as it pretends to be) exists in this unstable relationship to it.

Williams appeals to the point repeatedly: For example, he thinks that the Morality System embraces a very strong claim to intellectual self-sufficiency. It has a self-conception as inevitably higher or noble (such that it could not possibly be explained in terms of 'lower' values). Williams thinks both that this claim is false, and that this point further explains why Nietzschean genealogy is such an effective weapon to deploy against the Morality System.

Nevertheless, if Williams's reflections force us to give up on something – for example, morality's immunity to luck – we will experience that as a loss and not merely an intellectual one. Our starting point can be only the 'feelings and dispositions of judgement' that we, as historically situated selves, actually have: We are strongly motivated by the thought that justice requires us to 'exempt agents from (some) blame for (some) things done involuntarily' (Williams, 1995j, p. 243). The Morality System attaches considerable force to the observation that even if one is 'shunned, hated, unloved, and despised' as Williams puts it, at least one is not being blamed. Williams does not think that constitutes much of a reassurance.

Williams's answer to the question of why blame matters so much to us, and is so hegemonic over our other ethical reactions, appeals to its fundamentally universalising and democratising treatment in Kant's hands. But Kant's aspirations are ours as well: Williams argues that it is an attractive political project to remodel our social world as if Pelagianism were true. Blame, in this conception, focuses on 'what is available to the rational deliberator' and operates under the guarantee that 'the correct ethical demands are …. available to any rational deliberator' (Williams, 1995j, p. 246). In that sense the Morality System 'reassures' us. But Williams thinks that this reassurance is bogus.

Williams's critique begins from the phenomenology of how people think and feel about some 'usual' cases and extrapolates from that to some more dramatic, and unusual cases. In both kinds of case, these examples are freed from prior theory that dictates how we ought to interpret them. In other words, we are not as Kantian as neo-Kantian moral philosophers think we are or, perhaps, hope we are.

The point of the 'Gauguin' case, then, is to represent any person with 'definite and pressing' moral claims in his or her life who 'turns away' from them to pursue a ground project that seeks the genuinely worthwhile. 'Turns away', and not 'ignores': If this Paul Gauguin simply did not care that he was married, had children, and familial obligations, it would not be the kind of case that interests Williams. That would distort the example in line with the Morality System's insistence that the only two kinds of motivation are altruistic or egoistic. Gauguin the rampant egomaniac would not be a very interesting character. (Williams, 1995j, p. 244).

The conditions of Gauguin's success are clear, but 'whether he will succeed cannot, in the nature of the case, be foreseen' (ibid, p. 23). You might describe the choice as risky:

> If he fails then he did the wrong thing, not just in the sense in which that platitudinously follows, but in the sense that having done the wrong thing in those circumstances he has no basis for the thought that he was justified in acting as he did. If he succeeds, he does have a basis for that thought. (Williams, 1981c, p. 23)

Suppose we take ethics to have two core concerns: One's relation to oneself and the expression of one's values, and a general disposition to be able to explain and justify one's actions to others. For this fundamental project, Williams does not think that the second aim can be met. Even if Gauguin made the right choice, and was 'ultimately' justified, he could not have justified himself to others ('or at least to all others'). Those who were hurt by his choices will still have grounds for reproaching him even if he succeeds in terms internal to the project. Failure means that there is no justification for his choice; yet success does not let him off the hook, either.

Williams argues that this example threatens a general model of how we reason about practice (Williams, 1995j, p. 245). There is ex ante deliberation, then the problem of how, ex post, an agent may change their view of themselves in ways that also changes their view of that original deliberation. The question then is not, simply, how one might have done better: '[T]he question I want to press comes before that reflection' (Williams, 1995j, p. 245).

It is only in so far as one can control an outcome via one's deliberation that the agent can be held to the standards of rationality. If an outcome emerges that is not responsive to that, then from the standpoint of the Morality System it might as well be the product of the agency of another person – or akin to a natural event (Williams, ibid). Williams thinks that this restriction is 'importantly wrong' and a person's 'involvement' in an action goes beyond the quality of his or her ex ante deliberation. If the question is a completely general one about practical agency, then blame is key again, because the Morality System treats guilt as self-directed blame, which is restricted to 'the rational self-criticism of a deliberator' (Williams, 1995j, p. 246).

That does not match up to our ordinary ethical experience. In particular, it falsifies our ethical emotions: We criticise those whom we take to have 'the wrong ethical sentiments or none' (Williams, 1995j, p. 246). Morality tells us to discipline those reactions to align them strictly with the scope of blame. Blame is restricted to those not merely at fault, but at fault for being at fault: The reason on which they failed to act is supposedly in everyone's 'subjective motivational set'. The Morality System pressurises the very idea of agency to re-shape it as luck free – as 'escap[-ing] as far as possible from contingency' (Williams, 1995j, p. 246). We are, once again, identifying why the Morality System is obsessed with blame and cannot make sense of agent regret.

Williams thinks that his Gauguin example demonstrates that a person's projects may unfold through time making justification available only retrospectively. At the time of deliberation and decision, the justificatory reasons lie in the future. What counts as failing to achieve a given outcome has criteria for success and failure that are internal to the project concerned. It makes a difference, in Williams's view, if there is an outcome which contains no good art by Gauguin because he tried and failed to produce it, or because he sustained an injury which meant he never tried to paint at all (Williams, 1981c, p. 25).

This is another aspect of the example that stresses the importance of agent regret: Williams argues that failure, in cases such as these, is something that the agent has this special reason to regret in a way that marks off this kind of regret (Williams, 1981c, p. 27). A person can feel such regret 'only towards his own past actions (or, at most, actions in which he regards himself as a participant)' (ibid). First personally, things could have been different, because you could have acted differently. You can, indeed, regret things done in the past and that would put you in the same position as a third-personal observer of your life. But this is not agent regret, which involves the first person in how it is distinctively expressed.

The scope of agent regret goes beyond what one intends to the outcomes that one brings about as a result of what one intends. Even in the case of an accident, agents can – and we expect them to – have ethical sentiments that reflect their causal involvement in producing that outcome. A natural impulse is to want to make amends, but even here this general desire does not reflect one's first-personal involvement in the right way. Williams's test is whether or not an insurance payout would cover the case. If not, then there is some 'reparative significance' to trying to make amends. In any case, he takes the existence of agent regret to be a phenomenological insight into broader issues about the structure of freedom and responsibility.

3.2 Agent Regret and the Shape of a Life

Human agency reaches full rational expression in that which one's actions bring about; exposure to luck, and the possibility of agent-regret, both reflect that underlying fact:

> One's history as an agent is a web in which anything that is the product of the will is surrounded and held up and partly formed by things that are not, in such a way that reflection can go only in one of two directions: Either in the direction of saying that responsible agency is a fairly superficial concept, which has a limited use in harmonizing what happens, or else that it is not a superficial concept, but that it cannot ultimately be purified. (Williams, 1981c, p. 29)

Williams thinks that the Kantian attempt to 'purify' the concept has demonstrably failed. That leaves the second option: a consciously 'superficial' account of responsible agency. One of Williams's strongest motivations here is to make sense of ancient tragedy: who you are is shaped by what you have done – 'what in the world one is responsible for' (ibid, p. 30).

In the case of ancient tragedy, people are victims of tragic fate: By contrast, Gauguin (and Anna Karenina in the 'Moral Luck' paper) make voluntary decisions. That which unites these examples is that how things turned out, something beyond the agent's control, determines whether the agent ought to regret them. Thus, Williams denies the appropriateness of regimenting the ethical sentiments so that regret is the canonical third-personal emotion, remorse the canonical first-personal emotion, where the latter is appropriate only for what one has done voluntarily (Williams, 1981c, p. 30). It is the Morality System which insists on this regimentation.

In the case of moral conflicts, Williams argues that there can be rational regret for the action not carried out even if what one did was for the best – another denial of the Morality System's thesis that obligations cannot ultimately conflict. Regretting how things turned out is not the same as regretting one's action: In the conflict case, there is no impugning what one did, simply that it was impossible to respond to two conflicting demands. The same distinction applies to agent regret: You can feel agent regret towards an outcome and one's role in bringing it about without regretting one's action.

All this phenomenological evidence informs Williams's conception of the shape of a life. Lives, as temporally extended sequences of choices, are poorly modelled via an idealized sequence of rational choices each of which is justified at the time of decision. Williams argues that, on this view, regret about past cases, where bad decisions turned out well or good decisions turned out badly, can only be instances where the agent resolves to deliberate better in the future. This makes sense, Williams notes, if one is developing a policy for 'an ongoing class of cases' – for example, as a blackjack player does. But the sequencing matters: The goal is not to formulate a policy for every hand of cards in one's future. That is why Williams thinks it is an extra, optional, step to develop a conception of a temporally neutral rational life-plan, as in Rawls's work, which involves discounting only for distant probabilities (Rawls, 1971/1999, p. 358).

Williams's fundamental objection to this model is that it overlooks the idea that one's life has a shape: It instead treats oneself as a trustee for one's future self, hoping for an outcome where one's future self cannot rationally reproach one's earlier self (Williams, 1981c, p. 34). This ignores the insight that the shape of a life is determined by the fact that 'what one does and the sort of life one leads conditions one's later desires and judgements' (ibid.). The life choices of a Gauguin represent, for Williams, a dramatic instance of something he takes to be ubiquitous in human life:

> In these cases, the project in the interests of which the decision is made is one with which the agent is identified in such a way that if it succeeds, his standpoint of assessment will be from a life which then derives an important part of its significance for him from that very fact; if he fails, it can, necessarily, have no such significance in his life. (Williams, 1981c, p. 34)

In the ordinary conduct of life, avoiding regret is the same thing as resolving to take good decisions. By contrast, Williams identifies in these existential cases an asymmetry:

> If he succeeds, it cannot be that while welcoming the outcome he more basically regrets the decision. If he fails, the standpoint will be of one for whom the ground project of the decision has proved worthless, and this . . . . must leave him with the most basic regrets. (Williams, 1981c, pp. 36–37)

Such decisions are not simply very risky. They are focused on conditions of meaningfulness: Such fundamental projects include, amongst their ramifications, crucially the 'standpoint of retrospective assessment' itself (Williams, 1981c, p. 36). The agent, in taking her decision, adopted a project that aimed to ground her life as a whole; it follows that intrinsic failure here leads to these 'most basic' forms of regret (ibid, p. 36). How do these existential decisions threaten the claims of morality? There are several possible views here; I think it is helpful to identify which one is Williams's.

At a first pass, it seems that Williams is arguing that morality is less important in our lives than a broader set of claims that he identifies as those of 'the ethical'. That, however, is a multiply ambiguous claim because of the ambiguities in the word 'importance'. We might, for example, reduce the scope of moral considerations, giving them importance in that limited domain, while giving them less overall importance in a person's life. That is not, I think, Williams's view. I think the best interpretation of what he says is that – once again – there is an asymmetric dependence at work where not only is the scope of morality reduced, but it has the importance it has only because it depends on ethical considerations that are prior to it.

All of these arguments are underpinned by Williams's claim that the Morality System lives a hypocritical double life. Morality, on this view, can never make anything less than a claim to total supremacy over our ethical reasons (Williams, 1981c, p. 37). It also insists that the only reasons in opposition to its own are egoistic, or amoral (ibid, p. 38). That is why Williams complains that it is an inherently hegemonic idea that must, of its nature, misrepresent the complex phenomenology of our actual ethical experience. It is part of our ordinary experience that our lives have a 'shape', in William's sense, in a way that the Morality System fails to acknowledge.

3.3 Freedom of the Will

A corollary of the foregoing is that Williams thinks that we need to deflate the traditional problem of free will. It is the Morality System that freights our ordinary concept of voluntariness with a weight it cannot carry. It must be, from its perspective, a deep idea – a focal point for the absolute justice of Kant's implicit Pelagianism. However, when we turn to our ordinary conception of agency, we do not find a deep idea of human freedom; rather, a 'shallow' one.

Williams does not deny that it is a constitutive fact about an action that it be voluntary in the sense of 'an intended aspect of something done in a state of mind that is deliberately normal' (Williams, 1995j, p. 243). But this characterisation is 'essentially superficial' because the work is being done by the contrasting idea of the *involuntary*. It is the latter that the Morality System wants to 'deepen', because some things done involuntarily get a person off the hook from blame (partly or wholly) – again, in the interests of justice (ibid, p. 243).

Mature ethical agency involves this thought: A person 'recognizes that his identity as an agent is constituted by more than his deliberative self' (Williams, 1995b, p. 32). The relevant connection is between one's character and what one has brought about through one's action in a way that extends to the 'undeliberated', 'unforeseen', and 'unintended' aspects of action (Williams, 1995b, p. 32). By acknowledging these aspects as one's own, the agent responsibly acknowledges that some things she did were not what she intended. More ethically fundamental than the social mechanisms that hold one accountable is holding oneself responsible for these actions in a way one must acknowledge. That is a broader, more demanding ideal than that of being held responsible by some mechanism of public accountability.

Those public mechanisms have the aims of social control and cohesion (Williams, 1995b, p. 32). It is an evasion of responsibility if an ethically mature person holds themselves responsible only to those reductive public standards. Given his later sympathy with political republicanism, it is interesting that Williams does not think that his ideal of ethical maturity coincides with the highest form of political citizenship as collective self-authorship of the laws of the republic (Williams, 2002, chapter nine). A liberal politics requires only acknowledgement in a weaker sense: of holding each other to publicly known standards.

Beyond the political, and the public, we have the domain of responsibility for character within our personal relations to one another and the extent to which it can be shaped by reason. Here Williams appeals to a distinction between a moralising psychology versus a minimal one distinguishing how each treats the idea of freedom. Aristotle thought that a person who was unfree, for example, because of self-indulgence could be held responsible for the voluntary steps that led, cumulatively, to a loss of voluntariness. Bad character is not, Williams retorts, like addiction. In any case voluntary steps which, iterated, lead to addiction do not make the latter voluntary (Williams, 1995b, p. 27). Local control, however, Williams thinks is psychologically realistic. An individual's concern with 'mak[-ing] sense of his or her life' can be developed in the direction of Williams's own idea of the ethically mature agent.

Does that mean, then, that we are ultimately free? Williams thinks that is a bad question not least because it is framed, as the Morality System frames it, in 'all or nothing' terms. Our ordinary understanding is more nuanced than that: It typically treats freedom – rightly in Williams's view – as a matter of degree (Williams, 1995a, p. 3). Our ordinary concept of freedom seems, in that respect, closer to the philosophical view known as compatibilism.

Compatibilism thinks that free action is compatible with your actions being caused, in the right kind of way – caused by your beliefs, desires and character.

Williams argues that any compatibilist view must also accept that freedom comes in degrees because that which vitiates it is constraint via 'hostile agency'. In such cases person A threatens, or exerts force, on person B such that the latter cannot achieve her aim in action or does so at increased cost. Consider Aristotle's example of the sea captain who must throw a valuable cargo overboard in a storm or risk losing the ship. Is the captain responsible for his choice? The agent can, after all, choose and will be held responsible for this decision. Williams concludes we do not learn very much from such cases precisely because there is no loss of free will.

For him, the interesting point is that action under constraint is related in a special way to the conclusion that one *must* or *has to* do a certain thing (ibid). That is because he believes that any agent wants to protect the core identifications from which expressions of practical necessity flow. Their form expresses 'some of the most serious and responsible decisions we take' (Williams, 1995a, p. 5). That is why we are especially concerned when someone tries to substitute their intentions for our own: Being under someone else's power seems like a paradigm of unfreedom. (But we are still making decisions.)

Williams argues that our problem is not whether compatibilism and moral responsibility can coexist: Our problem is to understand whether choice is, as Williams puts it, a psychological or metaphysical notion. The point of the philosophical challenge of determinism is that it seems to make choice situations a sham: It cuts down the options available to the agent to one. Williams thinks that we do not need the dramatic threat of universal determinism to make the point. All we need is the idea that human actions can be fully explained by a strong form of philosophical naturalism. What range of actions presents themselves to the agent as deliberative alternatives that are open to him or her? Williams thinks that a generally naturalistic account of human action allows us to retain the basic range of the concepts we need. That fact, Williams avers, does not yet solve the real problem: a reconciliation of this range of concepts with our ethical concepts.

The crux of the issue, then, is the relation between our ordinary notion of responsibility and the philosophically inflected concept of blame re-shaped (for its own ends) by the Morality System. This philosophical conception of blame gives it, essentially, a forward-looking function – it must modify an agent's motives. As Williams notes, this is a curious combination of an intrinsic justification and an instrumentalist one – we value the practice of blaming for its own sake and for its overall point.

His first complaint is that we sell blame short by explaining it via its efficacy. Such an explanation would be inadequate (for legal philosopher Herbert Hart's reason) that it is only effective if the person blamed thinks that, qua reaction, is merited. If not, the agent merely resents being blamed.

Morality exaggerates the importance of blame and thereby makes it too central to ethical life. In particular, the Morality System has difficulty explaining why practical necessities are so important to us. It delivers us straight into this paradox: Accounts of free action, influenced by the moral psychology of blame, stress the condition that the agent 'could have done otherwise'. But this is precisely a condition absent from some of the actions most central to our practical identity and with which we are most deeply identified. What is distinctive about cases of practical necessity, when they stem from our deepest identifications, is that we do *not* want to have done otherwise. There is a general pattern to such claims about necessity:

> 'I must' implies 'I cannot not', and 'I had to' implies 'I could do nothing else'. . . .. responsibility does not entail 'I could have acted otherwise', and the search for some reconciling explication of that formula loses some of its urgency. (Williams, 1995a, p. 17)

Williams argues that if a person rightly concludes that he must do a certain thing then it is impossible, not that he should fail to do it, but that he should intentionally fail to do it. The word 'necessity', occurring here, expresses the agent's intention.

It is not the agent, third personally as it were, reporting some antecedent truth that limited her powers to decide. If that were the correct explanation, then the agent could not do the thing in question either intentionally or unintentionally.

> We can see ... how these various points hang together, if we take seriously the point that *statements of practical necessity express intentions*. (Williams, 1995a, p. 18, emphasis added)

In ordinary speech, we might say 'I am going to do x' which is tantamount to saying that if I deliberate, and come to a conclusion, then I can reasonably count on that bringing about a change in the world of which my agency is the cause. By contrast, Williams thinks, when I say 'I cannot do x' then there is a different implication, namely:

> [T]hat no possible world contains my acting in this way, if it contains me with these projects, and permits the general conditions for my projects to be expressed in action. (Williams, 1995a, p. 18)

Conclusions of practical necessity, then, express some of the deepest ethical demands on us, yet we do not insist, in these cases, on the condition for free action on which the Morality System most strongly insists.

Williams's overall diagnosis, then, is that nothing in our ordinary idea of freedom is incompatible with the idea that there is a naturalistic explanation of human action. The real problem is the incompatibility between the pressure that the Morality System puts on our psychological concepts and our ordinary notion of free agency. The important issue is neither naturalism, nor determinism, but the moralisation of basic psychological concepts such as choice.

Freed from the pressures generated by the Morality System, Williams's conclusion about freedom is optimistic:

> [I]f we bring our ethical ideas nearer to reality, then assuredly we shall find that they are consistent with naturalistic explanations of our choices and attitudes. *The will is as free as it needs to be* ... we have quite enough of [freedom] to lead a significant ethical life in truthful understanding of what that life involves. (Williams, 1995a, p. 19, emphasis added)

Given the centrality of character and its expression by action in Williams's overall conception, it is unsurprising that necessities grounded in character are of particular interest to him. I will turn next to the connections that he draws not between that idea and freedom, but between practical necessity and the idea of certain (in)capacities of character that are also revealing aspects of our ethical life.

3.4 Practical Necessity and Incapacities of Character

Williams thinks that it is part of our everyday ethical experience that an individual may conclude that 'a certain action is one that he must, or has to, do' (Williams, 1981f, p. 124). Williams was here influenced by a paper he admired, namely, Peter Winch's 'The Universalisability of Moral Judgement' (Winch, 1965). While 'ought' is a comparatively weak modality it can be used to express a practical conclusion – in Philippa Foot's helpful terminology, the 'verdictive' use of that term expresses an all things considered conclusion to practical deliberation (Foot, 1978).

Williams notes that it is not usually true that in successful cases of deliberation, there is only one thing I can do to realise my goal. (Even though alternatives may be more costly or violate some deontic constraint.) However, when they are all ruled out there is one thing I *must* do. He argues that there are 'serious cases' where the concept of necessity applies to our assumptions from which we deliberate: Some alternatives are 'impossible' for us. This fact can play an important role in deliberation. The deliberator can either express her conclusion as a practical necessity: 'I have to do x' (thus the alternatives are things she cannot do) or as a moral incapacity: 'I cannot do y or z, hence I must do x'.

This analysis allows Williams to isolate the case that interests him: This special sense of 'cannot': 'The cannot of practical necessity introduces a certain kind of incapacity' (Williams, 1981f, p. 128). The deliberator can recognise that he or she cannot do a certain thing, but the observer of that person can go a step further and acknowledge the category of the unthinkable:

> [T]hinking that something is unthinkable is not so direct a witness to its being
> unthinkable as is being incapable of thinking it. (Williams, 1981f, p. 129)

It does not follow that, if an agent is incapable of doing x in this sense, then she will not do it – but she will not do it intentionally. She might do it unintentionally – for example, through ignorance. These are incapacities of character, not literally what you physically cannot do. Physical incapacity is different; if I cannot lift a ton there is no event in the world that is my lifting a ton. Other psychological incapacities are being unable to do something if I know I am – such as walking on a tightrope over a steep drop. The world might contain this event but not if I know what I am doing:

> [I]n the pure cases of moral incapacity … it is not necessarily true that if
> I tried I would fail. If I tried, I might well succeed. The moral incapacity is
> revealed in the fact for the appropriate kind of reasons I will never try.
> (Williams, 1995d, p. 49)

The necessary asymmetry of most virtue terms means that we, the agent's community of appraisers, usually apply the virtue term to the agent whose ethical attention is outwards, on the practical question to hand.

But we, as appraisers, can also come to a judgement of your character based on what it occurred to you to do or that which was unthinkable for you. This is, for Williams, an important source of self-knowledge:

> Incapacities can not only set limits to character and provide conditions of it,
> but can also partly constitute its substance. To arrive at the conclusion that one
> must do a certain thing is, typically, to make a discovery – a discovery which
> is always minimally, and sometimes substantially, a discovery about oneself.
> (Williams, 1981f, p. 130)

Winch focused on Melville's novella, *Billy Budd*, and the judgement of the fictional Napoleonic sea captain 'Starry' Vere that he could live with the unjust condemnation of the saintly Billy Budd. It was a matter of military necessity that Vere sentence Budd to death for a killing that was not intentional. But, as it turned out, Vere found out via his decision that this was precisely something he couldn't live with: He dies, guilt-stricken, with Budd's name on his lips. A decision with which one is identified is one for which a person will be held responsible. In acknowledging that fact, the agent makes the action 'one's own' (Williams, 1981f, p. 130). Vere gets this decision horribly wrong; yet Williams also emphasises that this form of self-discovery is not in spite of, but because of, the agent's 'outward' focus on getting an ethical conclusion right.

Vere was not obsessing about his character but with what he had to do; his flawed deliberation led to his discovering something about himself he could not have found out any other way. Williams thinks that Winch identifies something important:

> The recognition of practical necessity must involve an understanding at once of one's powers and incapacities, and of what the world permits, and the recognition of a limit which is neither simply external to the self, nor yet a product of the will, is what can lend a special authority or dignity to such decisions. (Williams, 1981f, pp. 130–131)

This early paper foreshadowed the contents of *Shame and Necessity*, published in 1993. This book is an extended argument to the effect that, given that the ancient tragedians and ethicists can make better sense of such ethical experiences of practical necessity and the continued relevance of shame, there is every reason to reject a certain historiography of our own ethics. That claim – that ancient ethical thought was comparatively 'underdeveloped' compared to the modern moral consciousness – is yet another manifestation of the Morality System.

3.5 The Recovery of Ancient Ethics

Shame and Necessity is Williams's most extended act of historical retrieval. He begins by noting the use of the methods of cultural anthropology to make ancient Greek culture more distant from us; he concedes that we cannot share their world. But his study aims to uncover 'unacknowledged similarities between some Greek conceptions and our own' (Williams, 1993, p. 2). Our ethical modernity, far from affording us a superior standpoint on basic concepts of moral psychology, rather blinds us to these similarities (Williams, 1993, p. 3).

He thinks that we have sufficient grounds for rejecting the progressivist view that modern ethical conceptions stand to ancient Greek conceptions as sophisticated developments out of the comparatively 'primitive'. Williams openly acknowledges the difficulty of placing the Sophoclean tragedies at the centre of his discussion: We share neither a Sophoclean conception of the gods, nor of fate. His response is that 'we should look for analogies in our experience and our sense of the world in the necessities that they express' (Williams, 1993, p. 19).

Representative in Williams's discussion is the progressivist treatment of the work of Homer as representing an unsophisticated moral consciousness. Williams responds to the progressivist complaint that there is something 'missing' from 'Homer's man':

> What people miss, I suspect, is a 'will' that has these two features: it is expressed in action, rather than in endurance, because its operation is supposed itself to be a paradigm of action, and it serves in the interest of only one kind of motive, the motives of morality. (Williams, 1993, p. 41)

For Williams it is an insight, not a defect, of these Homeric texts that they do not involve a basic moralisation of psychology – the colonisation of explanatory categories of action by ethical ideas. That is, as we have seen, for Williams one of the primary distortions of our ethical thought by the Morality System.

On the contrary, ancient ethics makes better sense of the very facts to which Williams repeatedly draws attention in his critique of how that System distorts the concepts and categories of our moral psychology: 'There is not, and there could never be, just one appropriate way of adjusting these elements to one another' (Williams, 1993, p. 55). The concept of responsibility applies whenever an agent is a cause of an outcome. Williams begins his explanation of responsibility by setting aside cases of strict liability in law: For example, when an employer is held liable for the faults caused by employees. This is a special case where to undertake to do business in this way is to accept this prior and very general presumption of responsibility. For all other cases, we hold responsible only the agent who has caused the outcome.

Our modern conception of law, Williams thinks, plays a role in falsely legitimising the Morality System and its proprietary account of moral responsibility: To a considerable extent, he argues, the idea that the Greeks thought very differently from ourselves about responsibility, and more 'primitively', is an illusion generated by thinking only about the criminal law and forgetting the law of torts (Williams, 1993, p. 63).

We do argue, he notes, about harm or damage brought about by what was unintentionally done. The focus is not on fundamental conditions on responsibility; instead, the focus is on that which the agent's unintentional action caused – and that can simply be a matter of luck. The relevant difference between ancient Greek practice and our own does not depend on some deeper insight we have into moral responsibility but, Williams claims, on our different conception of the role of the state and a different conception of law (Williams, 1993, p. 65).

In particular, we have a political theory of freedom that seeks to preserve an individual's 'control over his or her life', as Williams puts it, that shapes a liberal conception of law. Our notion of responsibility is largely determined by our ideas of what it is for an individual to be treated fairly by the state. By contrast, the focus of ancient tragedy is not on the demands placed on an agent by impersonal third parties; rather, the demands placed on the agent by him or herself:

> The whole of *Oedipus Tyrannus*, that dreadful machine, moves to the discovery of just one thing, that he did it. We know that in the story of one's life there is authority exercised by what one has done, and not merely by what one has intentionally done. (Williams, 1993, p. 69).

Williams takes such examples to prove the importance, once more, of agent regret. In our modern world, as Williams notes, if you are affluent then your unintentional harm to others may be insured against (Williams, 1993, p. 70). But that need not exhaust their moral claims on you. He applies his criterial test again: Is an insurance payout enough? You may wreck your own life by things brought about unintentionally, of which you are the cause, where you simply accept that tragic fact (Williams, 1993, p. 70).

Ancient tragedy also gives us insight into the predicament of people who cannot live with what they have done. This is true even of those actions performed 'when not of sound mind' – even though in the plays Williams discusses it is divine intervention that causes the agents not to know what they are doing. Ajax, intending to take revenge for a wrong, is deceived by the gods into killing not his human enemies but a flock of sheep. Returned to 'sound mind' he is humiliated and shamed by what he has done and cannot live with it. Given his social identity and its need for acknowledgement in the eyes of others, he cannot go on after having carried out the deed, whether he acted intentionally or not (Williams, 1993, pp. 73–74). Motivated by anticipated shame, Ajax is not, Williams emphasizes, in the grip of 'heteronomous motivations' as the Morality System would classify them. Ajax fears shame in the eyes of another who is 'an internalized other' (Williams, 1993, p. 84). Ajax's reactions are culturally shared, in that other people would accept the same reason to be ashamed in their own life that Ajax perceives in his. But his life is different: He is a heroic warrior. It is that fact which makes his prospective shame more than he is prepared to live with.

Ajax concludes that he must end his life but, as Williams notes, he might equally think he must not: 'this is a type of ethical thought as far removed as may be from the concerns of obligation' (Williams, 1993, p. 74). Ancient tragic heroes, Williams concludes, can exemplify the point that

> the significance of someone's life and its relation to society may be such that someone needs to recognize and express his responsibility for actions when no one else would have the right to make a claim for damages or the right to do so. (Williams, 1993, p. 74).

Ajax's conclusion is not a categorical imperative of moral obligation; nor is it Kant's only other option, the hypothetical imperative that Ajax can 'go as he must go' if he wants to do so. The Kantian insists that this desire must be presupposed, somewhere, and this deep presupposition explains why, for the progressivist, the ancient philosophers and tragedians are not yet in the domain of modern morality.

Guilt is closer to the concerns of morality; Williams argues that shame and guilt are distinct. The person who is ashamed feels, as a whole person, exposed to the gaze of another and wants to disappear. Guilt, however, seems more pervasive. A person acts, or fails to act, in a way that incurs the anger and indignation of others, and the agent must make reparations or fear punishment. Shame elicits derision or contempt or avoidance in a way that diminishes an agent's self-respect (Williams, 1993, pp. 89–90). These moral emotions, then, seem to be filling complementary roles.

By one's actions, one can reasonably incur both shame and guilt; the deed can have 'authority over our own feelings' even in the case of the involuntary (Williams, 1993, p. 93). Agent regret can take the form of guilt. Shame, on the other hand, leads the agent to reflect on her moral identity: Who she is and what standards she seeks to live by. While the Morality System invites us to examine the relations between guilt and the voluntary, our ordinary ethical thinking takes it that the territory of shame is the aspect of our character that can lead to involuntary harms. For example, it is shameful to be so careless while driving that one involuntarily causes an accident. While guilt focuses on the victims of one's actions and reparations to them, the moral repair of our social relationship with them depends on shame and its connection to the agent's conception of herself as she relates to others (Williams, 1993, p. 94).

This contrast allows Williams to offer the following deracinated conception of virtue offered by the Morality System:

> [T]he truly moral self is characterless. In this picture, I am provided by reason, or perhaps by religious illumination (the picture owes much to Christianity) with a knowledge of the moral law, and I need only the will to obey it …. (This false picture is closely related to illusions …. such as a moralised basic structure of the mind and the search for an intrinsically just conception of responsibility.) (Williams, 1993, pp. 94–95)

For Williams, the crucial component missing from this picture is that it must include an internalised other that represents the essential sociality of reason. To insist, as his opponents do, that this is a form of heteronomy in motivation is also to insist that being a conduit of reason, alone, suffices for a person's autonomy. The rationalism underpins the 'characterless' moral self:

> But if we now think, plausibly enough, that the power of reason is not by itself to distinguish good and bad; …. then we should hope that there is some limit to these people's autonomy, that there is an internalised other in them that carries some genuine social weight. (Williams, 1993, p. 100)

Williams derives another corollary from ethical Cartesianism: If 'the criticising self is simply the perspective of reason or morality' – one way in which it is 'characterless' – then this fuels the idea of a perspective of complete rational autonomy (Williams, 1993, p. 159). This 'total critique' expresses an ideal of 'ultimate freedom' (p. 158). Williams uses this idea insightfully to diagnose the apparently inconsistent claim that ancient ethics is defective both by being too egoistic and yet too heteronomously concerned with the opinion of others.

His response to this charge begins from the point that shame plays the same essential role for ancient Homeric warriors as it does for us:

> [S]hame continues to work for us, as it did for the Greeks, in essential ways. By giving through the emotions a sense of who one is and of what one hopes to be, it mediates between act, character, and consequence, and also between ethical demands and the rest of life. Whatever it is working on, it requires an internalised other, who is not designated merely as a representative of an independently identified social group, and whose reactions the agent can respect. (Williams, 1993, p. 102)

Tragic characters are represented to us as experiencing a necessity to act in certain ways, a conviction that they must do certain things, and Williams connects this sense of practical necessity to the mechanisms of shame.

The source of the necessity is in the agent, via an internalised other whose view the agent can respect. Indeed, he can identify with this figure, and the respect is to that extent self-respect; but at the same time the figure remains a genuine other, the embodiment of a genuine social expectation. These necessities are internal, grounded in the *ēthos*, the projects, the individual nature of the agent, and in the way he conceives the relation of his life to other people's lives (Williams, 1993, p. 103). Mature ethical agency, in responding to this internalised demand, is not guilty of 'heteronymy'.

Towards the close of *S&N* Williams generalises not simply over the argument of that book but over his work as a whole. The hero of *S&N* turns out to be the ancient historian Thucydides (alongside the tragedians). Williams's discussion identifies a linchpin of his entire philosophy of ethics: What it is to have a naturalistically acceptable view of the basic psychological concepts we need to do ethics. In Williams's account Aristotle, for all his insights, is classed with Plato as a theorist who ethicises fundamental psychological concepts in a way that is explanatorily inadequate. They both – like Kant – take fundamental categories for the understanding of the mind as themselves basically ethical (Williams, 1993, pp. 43–45, pp. 160 ff; 1995f).

By contrast, Thucydides offers an explanatory perspective that is, on the one hand, not 'value-free' – it is an evaluatively engaged perspective. On the other hand, 'the psychology he deploys in his explanations is not at the service of his ethical beliefs' (Williams, 1993, p. 161). His goal

> is to make sense of social events, and that involves relating them intelligibly to human motivations, and to the ways in which situations appear to agents . . . .

> Thucydides' conception of an intelligible and typically human motivation is broader and less committed to a distinctive ethical outlook than Plato's . . .. The same is true in relation to Aristotle. (Williams, 1993, pp. 161–162)

There is an element of self-identification in Williams's admiration for the ironic, realist, historian who, alongside the ancient tragedians, does not in his writings represent an 'undeveloped' form of moral consciousness. On the contrary, its particular value is that it has not developed the obsessions of the Morality System.

4 The Fate of Moral Knowledge

As I noted at the outset of this Element, Williams thought that a great deal of philosophical energy was devoted to establishing the claim that ethics involves knowledge – as, for example, in Thomas (2006). Typically, for Williams, in his later work he asks whether those – such as myself – who defend moral cognitivism have sufficiently explained why we attach such importance to establishing its truth? Once again, the basic issue is the authority of moral reasons (Williams, 1995 l, p. 227).

To go back to his example: A university professor is being dragged out of her office by some uniformed thugs. In addition to telling them they are acting irrationally, the professor exclaims 'what you are doing to me is sadistic!'. Suppose she is right – her claim is true. What difference would this make? Williams always tried to deflate the importance of the issue of moral realism. This question, he thought, was inevitably accompanied by a complementary problem of moral scepticism (Williams, 2016). Williams thought that the effort devoted to scepticism about the objectivity of morality ought, instead, to have been focused on freeing ourselves from the Morality System. The latter makes a specious claim to moral authority; does moral cognitivism makes an equally specious claim to rational and moral authority?

This section will describe Williams's complex answer to that question. I will begin with what is at stake: How best to conceptualise the issue. This leads directly to Williams's perennial contrast between 'the ethical' and 'the scientific', which invited the (misleading) interpretation that he was an orthodox moral sceptic. If that was your framework for interpreting him, then it would have seemed odd that he demonstrated such sympathy with a wave of reformulations of moral realism developed by moral philosophers influenced by Wittgenstein. They drew our attention to ethical claims that use so-called 'thick' ethical concepts: Specific conceptualisations of the ways in which things are wrong, for example, by being *cruel* or *sadistic*, that both conceptualise them and connect such judgements to reasons for action (I will refer to concepts by italicising the terms that refer to them.) Williams's account of their work seemed, in many respects, supportive of their key arguments.

But only up to a point: Two of his distinctive claims then challenge this Wittgensteinian position. One was the contrast with the scientific – a contrast we can, I think, finesse from the perspective of the Wittgensteinian cognitivist (Thomas, 2006). More challengingly, Williams not only thought that an ethical outlook was a way of finding one's way around *a* social world rather than *the* social world, but also thought that there were arguments drawn from the social sciences and history to demonstrate that there is a plurality of such worlds, each drawing on its own conceptual repertoire, and that our ethical practices were proof of such diversity. The culmination of this argument was one of his most puzzling claims: That a given social group could achieve moral knowledge only then to lose it through reflection (Williams, 1985, chapter 8; Moore, 2003; Thomas, 2006). I will try to contextualise that argument to clarify Williams's 'non-objectivism' about the ethical.

4.1 Formulating the Issue of Cognitivism/Realism

I have already started to use some of the terms necessary to formulate the issue: objectivity, realism, and cognitivism. I will now explain how these terms are used before introducing a key concept – minimalism about truth (Wright, 1992).

The most general term on the list is objectivity. Williams thought that ethical objectivity involved two distinct issues (Williams, 1985, p. 132). One grounds a claim to ethical objectivity in our perspective as practical reasoners: There are some reasons that are necessary for any practically engaged agent. I have documented his multifaceted critique of this claim as developed, for example, by Nagel. The second issue grounds a claim to ethical objectivity in our perspective as theoretical reasoners: Those who seek to know, via inquiry, whether there really are moral facts.

Ought we to be realist about these domains? In speaking of 'domains' it has become true that philosophers are rarely realists, tout court, but realists about particular domains. For example, I hope that readers of this Element are realists about astronomy, but not about astrology. The realist claims that when we factually describe a particular domain, its existence and structure is independent of human minds (Williams, 1978, p. 64). The astronomer studies astronomical phenomena, whose existence and nature are independent of our beliefs about them. The astrologer is doing something else: Presenting putative facts not with the aim of informing, but of entertaining, or doing something else that does not involve claims about planetary influence on human character being factually true.

The next term of art here, cognitivism, introduces the idea of the kind of mental content expressed when we make some of our ethical judgements. People seem, on the face of it, to make remarks like 'I know for a fact that Hitler was a cruel man'. The verb 'know' suggests that this sentence, at least across one of its dimensions, expresses the mental state of knowledge. By contrast, a wide range of moral philosophers from emotivists, to expressivists, to prescriptivists deny that ethical judgements express beliefs (or knowledge). These statements do something else: Express simple emotions, or complex structured sets of attitudes, or issue prescriptions and self-addressed imperatives.

Objectivity is the generic idea; realism a species; cognitivism a way of articulating the commitments of realism. What role is played here by the concept of truth? From this necessarily brief sketch, it seems that truth will play an important role in this debate. For example, it seems as though the astronomer's claims are true to the facts while the astrologer's claims are not. Williams, however, later endorsed the view called minimalism about truth (Williams, 1995 l). This is, in one respect, a negative thesis: Truth is not the sort of thing about which one can develop a theory (neither explanatory nor metaphysical). When we attach 'is true' to a sentence we are using a predicate, but we add nothing to the content of the sentence. All the interest, then, is shifted back onto what it is to assert that sentence in the first place.

In an important late paper 'Truth in Ethics', Williams unpacks what he takes the consequences of the adoption of minimalism about truth for the debate over moral realism. It prioritises the point of the practices within which we regiment our statements to substantiate the minimalists' ambitious view of 'syntax' (Wright, 1992; Williams, 1995 l, p. 230). Adopting minimalism opens up the broad range of issues that Williams later discussed, notably in *T&T*, not about truth, rather, the values of truthfulness (ibid.). This relates back to his commitment to Enlightenment values which, in this context, involve such values as 'the authority of knowledge, the value of honest inquiry' (Williams, 1995 l, pp. 232–233). One problem for the moral realist is that she thinks what really matters is being able to discern truths about values and that, for Williams, misses the point. The point is whether we live in a culture in which people responsibly tell the truth about anything and not merely ethics.

The moral cognitivist can, I think, happily accept minimalism about truth. I think he or she can happily accept Williams's shifting of the focus of the debate to the internal rational discipline of those practices in which our ethical concepts have their home. But, most of all, the cognitivist welcomes Williams's recognition of an important class of ethical concepts the phenomenology of which makes a prima facie case that cognitivism is true: thick concepts.

4.2 Wittgensteinian Arguments from Thick Concepts

In my extension of Williams's example of the professor being dragged away by the police I added both her claim to know that her attackers are sadistic and her choice of that concept. *Sadistic*, we might say, is a concept that tells us more about the actions of the wrongdoers than the fact they are doing wrong. Central to Williams's discussion of moral realism is his account of thick ethical concepts: An idea that he traces back to Wittgenstein, but where the immediate point of transmission to him was 'a seminar in the 1950s' given by Philippa Foot and Iris Murdoch (Williams, 1985, p. 218, n.7).

The point of the distinction is this: Thin concepts, such as *good*, *bad*, *right*, and *wrong* tell us very little about the circumstances of their application. *Sadistic*, *courageous*, and *uplifting* do give us more determinacy: specificity and concrete detail about the circumstances in which they are applied. Furthermore, when the latter class of concepts are used in judgements, Williams tells us that they can be both 'world-guided' and 'action-guiding' (Williams, 1985, pp. 140–141).

The rationale for this distinction is to cause problems for any naive distinction between facts and values (Williams, 1985, p. 134). Suppose a guide is describing a cathedral to a group of tourists. In describing the beam across two columns as an 'architrave' she is informing them of a fact; in describing the beam as 'an elegant architrave' she seems to be doing exactly the same thing. There is a true sentence which ascribes an evaluative (aesthetic) property which is embedded in the speech act of describing.

The anti-realist, of any stripe, will express her unhappiness with this formulation. Yes, those may be the surface appearances of how we think and speak. But there is a difference between descriptive and evaluative properties which maps on to a distinction between descriptive and evaluative meaning. In taking thick concepts at face value, we are buying in to this misleading apparent fusion of description and evaluation. Such concepts ought to receive a philosophical analysis: They are a combination of two factors, one evaluative, and one descriptive. Had the tour guide been more explicit – perhaps a student of Dick Hare's – she would have added 'of course, by calling the architrave 'elegant', I was prescribing it to you. I was commending it in the light of a presupposed evaluative standard which makes some of its descriptive features relevant to its evaluation'.

The pushback from philosophers influenced by Wittgenstein is this: This proposed two-component analysis cannot be carried out (McDowell, 1985; Wiggins, 2000, pp. 185–211). For any expression that uses concepts, we can separate out its intension and its extension. The former has various theoretical articulations: For now, let's call it the expression's 'meaning'. The latter are the properties picked out by an expression with that meaning.

Take the thick concept *cruel*: What do all its instances have in common? The defender of thick concepts adds: Nothing that is not already apparent to those who share the evaluative interest in using the concept with its users. Without this shared interest, the list of things picked out by thick concepts – its extension – will look like an incoherent jumble. The list will seem shapeless unless you share the concept user's evaluative interest that led them to use this concept in the first place (Williams, 1985, p. 142). The two-factor theorist's project of analysing away thick ethical concepts into substantive, but descriptive concepts and thin evaluative concepts cannot be carried out.

If minimalism takes us back to the surface appearances of ethical phenomenology, and those appearances include the use of terms like 'know', 'fact', and 'assert', then what more could the cognitivist want? Williams seems to concede to cognitivism everything that it needs simply by recognising the class of judgements that use thick concepts. But Williams does not stop there – in ways I will now explain.

4.3 The Scientific and the Ethical

A trap for Williams's commentators is that, in spite of his protestations that he wants to break from the traditional question of moral realism, Williams does use the categories of 'the scientific' and 'the ethical'. Furthermore, he does so because he thinks we have moved beyond any naive formulation of the fact versus value distinction – and thick concepts played their phenomenological role in having achieving that. Yet does not that distinction recur in the way in which Williams uses his own pair of phrases? He seems to end up as an ethical sceptic all the same.

The grounds for saying this are that Williams defends a form of scientific realism: Science is an institution for acquiring knowledge where it can reasonably expect to be everything that it seems to be. It offers us a conception of the world 'to the maximum degree' independent of our perspective and its distinctive peculiarities (Williams, 1985, p. 139). It offers us a limited degree of self-transcendence. But this is not the chimera of a point of view from nowhere at all. It is simply that the most fundamental sciences transcend that which is distinctive of the human point of view.

Williams does not believe that the concepts and categories we need to conduct the most fundamental scientific inquiries – those of basic physics – are the only concepts and categories we need to explain the reflective activity of doing science (even doing physics). He does not think that the scientific worldview explains itself solely using its own most basic, non-perspectival concepts, in some act of reflexive completion whereby it explains its own generation and acceptance using only its own concepts.

The careful claim Williams makes is about scope: Some of our representations of the world are maximally non-perspectival. That does not mean that our representations about representations have the same feature (Williams, 1985, p. 140). He later came to regret some incautious suggestions in his book on Descartes that an absolute conception implied this kind of physicalist worldview (Williams, 1978, 1995k, p. 209). It does not.

Even so, the ethical sceptic thinks that there is enough in Williams's work to motivate scepticism. True: This characterisation of the contrast highlights how the scientific and the ethical have different purposes. The latter, using repertoires of primarily thick (and some less thick) ethical concepts, is how we construct the social worlds into which we are acculturated. They are ways, as Williams likes to put it, of finding our way around some social world or other. It is important that these socio-cultural worlds, too, are the subject matter of the social sciences. However, the absolute conception of the world claims that, at the limit, we can form a conception of the world, not a world.

For the sceptic, that is all we need to recast Williams as a traditional sceptic about moral realism – forget everything he says about thick concepts and minimalism. All we need, to forge an invidious contrast between the scientific and the ethical, is what he says about explanation. The crucial paragraph is in *ELP*:

> In a scientific inquiry there should ideally be convergence on an answer, where the best explanation of the convergence involves the idea the answer represents how things are; in the area of the ethical, at least at a high level of generality, there is no such coherent hope. (Williams, 1985, p. 136)

This is why, a page earlier, Williams claimed that 'science has some chance of being more or less what it seems . . . . . . while ethical thought has no chance of being everything it seems' (Williams, 1985, p. 135). That certainly sounds like a sophisticated form of scepticism!

I do not think, however, that we need to read Williams this way. This argument uses a specific conception of explanation. Suppose that scientific knowledge is of a world that exists anyway. Because, on Williams's view, this (first order) knowledge is maximally non-perspectival, it is not from any point of view in particular. Of course, it was accessed via a point of view. In explaining that fact, we are going to use all kinds of perspectival knowledge about our scientific practices, institutions and methods. [11] But the best reflective explanation of scientific knowledge 'directly vindicates' it, to use Adrian Moore's helpful expression (Moore, 2007).

---

[11] Williams is clear that this is not a delimitation of knowledge; rather of scientific knowledge. We can know all kinds of perspectival facts (ibid, p. 139).

By contrast, our reflective understanding of ethical knowledge has to view it as answerable to two dimensions of assessment. One is its articulation, via thick concepts, as both world guided and reason-giving. The other dimension is the social world within which it is articulated. It is accessed via some social world or other, because that is a presupposition of having the sets of concepts available that any given society possesses. That presupposition is the subject matter of our best social scientific understanding of ethical knowledge because it is perspectival through and through: It is always from some point of view.

Furthermore, this explanation takes as its subject matter what ethical agents know, without itself directly endorsing that knowledge. An engaged social scientist stands close enough to our ethical practices to make sense of them while being disengaged enough genuinely to explain them without simply repeating the first-order knowledge being explained (Moore, 2007). The scientific case was not like that: A person tried truthfully to know about the world as it is. She succeeded, so the best explanation of her success was that she came to know the world as it is. Her social world enabled her to make this judgement, but it is not part of the best explanation of her making it. Williams is entertainingly scathing about the 'strong school' in the sociology of science which, for example, claims that quarks are 'socially constructed' via 'the remarkable assumption that the sociology of knowledge is in a better position to deliver truth about science than science is to deliver truth about the world' (Williams, 2002, p. 3).

One strategy that the cognitivist can take to undermine this argument is to reject Williams's view of science as reflecting the aspiration to absoluteness. The other strategy is to accept the contrast, but argue that it is not damaging to the aim of defending the idea of ethical knowledge. If there is merely one core stock of ethical concepts, then we do not need to introduce a plurality of individuable social worlds into our explanation of ethical knowledge. Both Williams, and the cognitivist, have to say more.

4.4 Modernity, Reflection, and the Loss of Moral Knowledge

The idea that our ethical ideas can be indirectly, rather than directly vindicated is one that the moral cognitivist wants to cling to in the face of Williams's distinction between the scientific and the ethical. But he or she is not out of the woods. Because, on the one hand, Williams acknowledges that there is something distinctive about thick ethical concepts – just as the cognitivist claims. But this distinctiveness creates special problems. If there are such concepts, then how does a social scientist understand them when she explains social and historical change?

Williams consistently argued that how many thick concepts there are for a society to draw upon does not depend on philosophical accounts of them. Everything we know about human cultures tells us that there have been changes in social structures and societal outlooks – including, importantly, evaluative outlooks. To use another characteristic Williams idea, a repertoire of thick concepts *expresses* such an outlook. And it is the evolution of our societies in history that tell us how many thick concepts we have – not philosophy or ideology.

This point is deployed to attack the cognitivist's view that the idea of convergence on an ethical truth that can be substantively explained is just as available in ethics as it is in science (Williams, 1985, p. 140). The way this critique proceeds is via a thought experiment: That of a hypertraditional society where people use thick concepts to make ethical judgements and thereby acquire moral knowledge *that they then lose* (Williams, 1985, pp. 145–147). This is, to put it mildly, a puzzling argument.

To this point Williams has, like his Wittgensteinian interlocutors, 'start[- ed] with the thick' (Williams, 1995 l, p. 234). He consistently rejects the two-component reductive analysis of thick concepts offered by the ethical expressivist or prescriptivist (ibid). But he then seems to undercut his own argument using the example of the hypertraditional society where knowledge is displaced by reflection. This process of displacement is always, in Williams's explanation, a displacement of the thick by the thin where judgements using thin concepts are not world guided and hence not candidates to be known.

We are to imagine this hypertraditional society becoming more *modern*, in Williams's proprietary sense, whereby it is more pervasively reflective. Members of this society, Williams argued, now find themselves cut off from the knowledge that they used to have (Williams, 1985, p. 147). Reflection need not have this effect; but, if it does, then these judgers are in the odd situation of being unable to be both reflective and knowers. Yet they can see that their previous judgements were knowledge. The process of reflection may go into reverse: Perhaps the knowledge will be recovered. But not in the light of reflection.

Williams claims we can think about the activities of the ethical thinkers in the hypertraditional society in one of two ways: one, objectivist, construal sees them as finding out a local truth about the ethical – coming to know things. But this local knowledge must have general implications, in just the same way that an anthropologist who concludes that a society's magical practices really do contain causal claims about the way the world works will see the local claims as having these general implications.

A contrasting non-objectivist view sees these claims as merely ways of finding one's way around a social world. In a characteristic combination of Williams's irony and a rhetorical flourish, he argues that only on the non-objective model can we secure the view that the hypertraditionalists know. That is because in the objective model, the local claims have reflective implications that can unseat the original knowledge (Williams, 1985, p. 148). The non-objective understanding of the hypertraditionalists does not attribute to them these implications of reflection. Reflection can, not must, cause more local ethical knowledge to be lost. In the next section, we can see that when the thick is supplanted by the thin, and we try to develop ethical theories on that basis, we do not restore knowledge in that way either.

How could people lose the knowledge they once had? People use repertoires of thick ethical concepts from a specific 'evaluative outlook' and loss of that outlook cuts those people off from those concepts; yet as Adrian Moore notes 'they can still understand the outlook, and indeed the concept, just as an anthropologist or a historian can understand an evaluative outlook, which he or she does not share' (Moore, 2003, p. 344) Williams, qua philosopher of social science, insisted on the possibility both that judgements using thick concepts can express moral knowledge and that they can be understood by a sympathetic but non-identified observer who takes up an 'ethnographic stance'. [12]

The example of the hypertraditional society pulls apart two of Williams's thoughts about thick ethical concepts. The outlooks from which they are articulated are ways of finding one's way around a social world. Yet two people in the same world might become aware of a clash of evaluative outlooks – Williams always cited Oscar Wilde's remark that 'blasphemy' was not a word of his – and now we have to understand how two people with conflicting sets of thick concepts can both have knowledge. Answerability to the world is, after all, one aspect of the use of thick ethical concepts. Williams remarks that historical change can estrange an individual or group from a concept:

> To give it up, lose hold on it, or simply drift away from it, as modern societies in the past two centuries or less have, for instance, done one or more of those things in connection with the concept of *chastity*. (Williams, 1985, p. 207, fn. 12)

One way to explain what is happening here involves the idea of presuppositional failure: Individuals, or societies, are subject to processes of social change, which displace thick concepts, or groups of them, as evaluative outlooks change. Unproblematically, this makes some judgements unavailable that were available before because it was a presupposition of making them that certain concepts were accessible. [13]

---

[12] Can we not combine this social scientific explanation with an evaluative principle to offer a reductive two component analysis of thick concepts? Williams argues 'no': see Thomas (2006) pp. 151–152.

[13] As Moore helpfully notes '"True" and "False" do not apply to concepts' (Moore, p. 352).

But another way to make the same point is that Williams agrees with his Wittgensteinian fellow travellers that thick ethical concepts are an amalgam of world-guidedness and action-guidingness. They are not, then, capable of purification into solely theoretical concepts (Moore, p. 353). Accepting them is to accept an evaluative outlook, which is also to undertake practical commitments of reason-giving and, one might add, patterns of feeling.

The ethnographer or historian writing about Edwardian England who seeks to understand both Oscar Wilde's evaluative outlook and that of the social conservatives whom he scandalised might be able to see the occupants of both outlooks as capable of knowledge. Yet the joint occupation of the two evaluative standpoints is irreconcilable precisely because these are not two ways of carving up a non-evaluative reality or even two ways of carving up evaluative reality. That reduces the exercise to one of pure theory. It would leave out the connection between thick conceptualisations, reason-giving, and action. We are discussing two evaluative ways of life.

That is why our envisaged social scientist must be capable of a sympathetic, but non-identified, point of view from which both claims to knowledge are not known by the social scientist qua scientist. But she knows something – from her perspective in history or sociology – that entails the truth of what each of the two parties knows (Moore, 2003, pp. 348–349). This does not mean that our envisaged social scientist takes up the fully internal perspective of either party – again, not *qua* social scientist. Her explanation entails what the conflicting parties know and she knows her explanation to be true. But, ex hypothesi, it does not directly vindicate what each party knows. How could it? So there is nothing here to encourage the sceptic: This is merely how any social scientific account of the ethical must work.

The cognitivist remains uneasy: Williams's position makes sense. But making sense is not the same as being plausible. How can Williams share so many assumptions with the cognitivist yet formulate the challenge of his non-objectivism? Of course, there are reasonable disagreements within ethics which mean that people vary in which concepts they use. But why is this specific point being exaggerated into a fundamental clash of evaluative outlooks – unless the influence of MacIntyre's *After Virtue* has led Williams astray?

The cognitivist is worried that Williams's fable of the hypertraditionalists re-imports the kind of foundationalism about justification that I noted in Section 1 (Thomas, 2006). How, from the fact of piecemeal social change, do we end up with a model of a group of concept users attempting to vindicate their entire ethical outlook from some perspective wholly outside it?

This takes us to the crux of the issue – and why Williams does not really think this is an important issue at all, rather, a candidate for deflation. In a later paper, Williams takes a paradigmatic cognitivist claim: The example of a group of hooligans who set fire to a cat (Williams, 1995 l). He comments that 'the boys do a wanton and hideous thing to the cat' – thereby using two thick ethical concepts. David Wiggins, on behalf of cognitivism, claims that there is 'nothing else to think' but that the boys' act was cruel. Williams demurs:

> True, if you use the concept 'cruel', there is nothing else to think but that their behaviour was cruel. But there is nothing in the situation, or in the discourse of . . .. other people, that can recruit somebody into using the concept 'cruel' if they don't already. (Williams, 1995 l, p. 237)

For the cognitivist, this is a puzzling remark. They offer an account of virtuous people, and the evaluative features to which their virtues are a response, that stand in a (virtuously) circular relationship. They see no way of unpacking this further. How could a virtuous person see this situation, be thinking of it correctly, but not see it as cruel?

Williams responds: There is no one set of thick ethical concepts that all ethical judgers, as such, can be guaranteed to have. His earlier argument is restated: We inhabit some social world or other, each structured by its own repertoire of concepts, and there is no core set that all social worlds share. He accepts that the latter claim is the one that the cognitivist is most likely to want to defend. Differentiating two versions of the claim, Williams contests both the ways in which the cognitivist tries to shore up his or her position.

The first version claims that there is a single, unitary, set of thick ethical concepts (correlated with a set of virtues) and when evidence to the contrary is presented proponents of the view simply dismiss it. Williams was personally amused by a researcher he met who was adapting Thomas Aquinas's list of virtues to our modern conditions. This is the basis of the oblique reference in 'Truth in Ethics' to the 'sociologically optimistic' view that we can, via a 'large jump', move from Aquinas's social world to 'late twentieth-century Los Angeles' – which is where this researcher happened to be located while working with Philippa Foot (Williams, 1995 l, p. 241). Does a table of virtues drawn up by a Dominican monk in the thirteenth century just need 'adjustment' to modern conditions? Williams thought not.

The second version of a cognitivist defence claims that while there are, in Williams's words, 'undeniable' facts about 'historical and social variation', this has a deep explanation in terms of a core set of concepts, which receive different cultural expressions. This would have to be combined with an account of moral error. That attracts a different sceptical response from Williams:

> Perhaps it's possible that some such structure might emerge. But I still doubt
> it. I also doubt to what extent it would be other than an ethical project . . . .
> [N]o such theory now exists. To pretend that it does is simply bluff.
> (Williams, 1995 l, p. 242)

My own view – both when I worked with Williams and now – is that this represents a set of challenges to cognitivism and not a list of fatal defects (Thomas, 2006). The onus is on the cognitivist to say more to address these well-motivated concerns about the final defensibility of cognitivism.

Whatever one's view we are at least in a position to identify what is at stake between Williams and the moral realist. The latter thinks that, using the resources of the very social sciences that Williams has identified, there can be a reasonable explanation of moral disagreement framed in terms of basic points of agreement. That explanation need not, itself, simply endorse the knowledge that it explains. Those who believe that evaluative outlooks express sets of thick ethical concepts do not want to give up on the idea that they have some correct social scientific explanation. But nor do they accept the disaster scenario encapsulated in the fable of the hypertraditionalists. They contest Williams's history: There is enough agreement reasonably to frame our disagreements in just the way that MacIntyre argued was true within the one tradition he favoured. But that is because, for that tradition alone, MacIntyre had a different model for moral knowledge than the foundationalist model he applied to everyone else's tradition.

I will break off the argument between Williams and the cognitivist at this point: The latter will level against Williams's argument the verdict possible in Scottish courts of 'not proven'. In any case – and typically – Williams had moved on. In his later papers on this topic, Williams turned to the question of the value of truthfulness – that is the point that he thinks the moral cognitivist really ought to be concerned about (Williams, 1995 l).

The point of appealing to thick concepts, one that goes beyond the minimalist surface of the sentences that express them, is that they are a natural entry point for the idea that in ethics we have a lot of knowledge. If the point of that concept is to flag up reliability on the part of other ethical judges, we can form a conception of ethical expertise which is not modelled on that of the theoretical expert. Perhaps a better word would be insight: A 'helpful advisor', as Williams puts it, 'who can see that something falls under a certain thick concept' (Williams, 1995 l, p. 235).

Discussing the enterprise of ethical theory, in the next section, we will see that Williams contrasts it with a 'phenomenology of the ethical life'. It is part of that phenomenology, he thinks, that an advisor is not really in the business of telling you about the truth directly:

> [H]e may be able to show you by his discourse that [a] moral outlook will help
> you, will make your life more of a life, will set you free, and this can be true of
> other projects which are not assessed primarily in the dimension of the true.
> (Williams, 1995 l, p. 236)

Williams anticipates the realist's protest against this argument: 'You may think 'a life worth living' is itself an ethical concept that involves the notion of the truth' (ibid.) I don't think Williams disagrees: He just holds, simply, that the realist has the argument backwards (in a typical way). The cognitivist is so focused on establishing that we have moral knowledge that she has failed to explain why this is important in the first place.

5 Anti-Theory

Is there such as thing as a distinctively practical use of reason? Two answers have emerged so far: If reason were practical, we could defend the word 'distinctively' by defending the claim of essential first personality. Secondly: reason is practical *because there are thick concepts* (Moore, 2007). We make judgements which deploy thick concepts, and they have two features: They are world-guided and action-guiding (and hence reason-giving). Under appropriate conditions, we can both know things and be given reasons. Certainly, Williams thought that in a pervasively reflective modern society, there are pressures on those of our thick ethical concepts that remain. But enough remains to sustain the social phenomenon of 'confidence' in our ethical outlook (Williams, 1985, 1995k, pp. 207–210; Fricker, 2000; Thomas, 2006, pp. 153–157; Moore, 2007).

This section focuses on a further point: Williams's claim that when we lose thick concepts, via social or historical change, they are supplanted by thin ones. Thus, a further source of pressure on our thick concepts comes from within philosophy itself. Not only is it of no help in the task of living reflectively in the light of our commitment to truthfulness; it can damage our prospects of doing so. This is the primary reason why Williams was opposed to the construction of ethical theories.

He argued that this endeavour is misguided in several ways. Typically, it denies the essential first personality of practical reasoning. This is clearly so when it takes up an impartial perspective that requires the ethical agent to view herself as if she were another (Thomas, 2024). This reflective turn is based on a false and misleading analogy between our theoretical conception of the world and our practical relation to it. That false analogy is captured, for Williams, by Sidgwick's image of ethical objectivity as aspiring to the 'point of view of the universe' (Williams, 1995g).

Secondly, if our pervasively reflective societies see repertoires of thick ethical concepts dwindle over time, the theorist does not deprecate that fact.

She welcomes it. Williams summarises his fundamental objection to the enterprise of theory:

> Theory looks characteristically for considerations that are very general and have as little distinctive content as possible . . .. But critical reflection should seek for as much shared understanding as it can find on any issue. . . .. Theory typically uses the assumption that we probably have too many ethical ideas, some of which may turn out to be mere prejudices. Our major problem now is that we have not too many but too few, and we need to cherish as many as we can. (Williams, 1985, pp. 116–117)

The third error of the theorist is a lack of self-awareness: Her misguided projection of a model of theoretical reasoning into the domain of the practical is an error she cannot recognise because of the ahistoricism of her method. This 'ethics of inarticulacy', as Charles Taylor memorably labels it, cannot recognise the influence of the Morality System on the enterprise of theory (Taylor, 1989). Williams's diagnosis is that identifying it requires the method of genealogy: a method not part of the theorist's toolkit.

These compounding errors lead to yet another. Sir Peter Strawson once wrote of an 'Homeric Struggle' in the philosophy of language (Strawson, 1971). There is a parallel struggle in metaethics between those who take themselves to be developing a metaphysical theory of the right-making properties of actions and those who are committed to Williams's psychologistic constraint on reasons.

Members of the former camp tend to be unimpressed by Williams's work; following the lead of Eugene Bales, they disdain the moral psychology of action (Bales, 1971). Their self-conception is that of metaphysicians: Their task is to formulate a theory of reasons for an agent via a theory of the right-making properties of actions. Such theorists do not deny the need for a supplementary theory of an agent's reasons, but that is not their primary concern.

If this is your view, then Anscombe's injunction to stop doing ethics until we have an adequate account of ethical psychology will seem misplaced (Anscombe, 1958). So, indeed, will Williams's vignettes – primarily in 'A Critique of Utilitarianism' – that focus on agents who have to navigate important ethical choices: that, says the theorist, is no concern of mine *qua theorist* (Williams, 1973b). Perhaps it is an encouraging fact for this metaphysician that the ethical psychology of agents is highly plastic. Mill, a leading utilitarian, thought that the results of a naturalistic psychology of ethical development saw people as capable of accepting any set of norms whatsoever (Mill, 1961/1998, chapter III). [14]

This kind of theorist will see no connection between the enterprise of theory, our historically conditioned dependence on thin ethical concepts, and the kind

---

[14] See also Williams (1995f).

of ideology critique represented by Williams's objections to the Morality System. This is doubly unfortunate, because Williams believed that theoreticians were merely working out the consequences of mistaking the concerns of that system to be the truth about the ethical. The reductionism of the Morality System is not earned. The ethical theorist helps herself to the Morality System's reductionist approach to our ordinary ethical thinking. They do so to make the task of theoretical reduction seem easier than it is.

5.1 Theory, For and Against?

Williams rejects of all forms of ethical theory. Theories contribute to the erosion and displacement of thick ethical judgements; they replace conceptualisations in which we ought to have confidence with deracinated false equivalents in which we ought to have none. Theory takes itself to represent an Enlightenment spirit of critique when it simply perpetuates the false claims of the Morality System. And the enterprise of theory works in just the same way as the Morality System itself: It is asymmetrically dependent on the very ethical materials it falsifies and misrepresents in the name of critique in the guise of 'scientific progress'. [15]

Williams's most extended discussion of the motivations of the theorist is in *ELP*:

> I want to say that we can think in ethics, and in all sorts of ways, unless our historical and cultural circumstances have made it impossible – but that *philosophy can do little to determine how we should do so*. (Williams, 1985, p. 74, emphasis added)

We may be unfortunate and find ourselves in a historical context where 'thinking' in ethics has been made impossible. If we are fortunate enough not to be in that position, that is not itself a philosophical issue. This is because it is the very possibility of philosophical reflection about ethics that is at stake. Yet, even so, in those propitious circumstances we need to live reflectively in the light of the truth in a way that does not seem to draw on the distinctive resources of philosophy. Those resources, in the hands of theorist, are primarily those of building abstract models that use only thin ethical concepts.

It follows that, for Williams, whether philosophy supplies any 'tests' for ethical thinking is a question that has to be open. That is because the availability of such tests varies from one cultural and historical context to another

---

¹⁵ See, for example, Parfit's discussion of how the 'history of ethics' is 'only just beginning' because 'Non-religious ethics is the youngest and least advanced' of the sciences (Parfit, 1984, p. 453)

(Williams, 1985, p. 74). In the right circumstances there can, he believes, be ethical reflection and progress, but not using the methods of philosophy.

At one point Williams describes an alternative to theory, namely, 'a phenomenology of the ethical life':

> Such a philosophy would reflect on what we believe, feel, take for granted; the ways in which we confront obligations and recognize responsibility; the sentiments of guilt and shame. (Williams, 1985, p. 93)

This will strike his readers as a self-portrait: '[T]his could be a good philosophy', Williams continues, 'but it would be unlikely to yield an ethical theory' (ibid.). It would have started from the right place, within ethical life as it is lived, but it would not be focused, as theory is, on 'just one aspect of ethical experience', namely, its cognitive structure as a set of beliefs. (By analogy with a scientific theory.) Ethical theory, on this understanding, 'in part provides a framework for our beliefs, in part criticises or revises them' (ibid). Williams is sceptical that they have the intellectual authority to do so (Williams, 1985, p. 99). In the next sections, I will discuss Williams's critiques of two major forms of ethical theory in the academic literature. Since both of these theories are impartialist, it is helpful to begin with this general target for his objections.

5.2 Mind the Gap: The Critique of Impartiality

The two most important options for the theorist, at the time when Williams wrote, were consequentialism and contractualism, both of which are impartialist theories. Much philosophical work adjudicates the conflict between them; Williams thinks both are incorrect. Which of his arguments apply to this generic impartialism?

First, we can set aside an irrelevant issue: Williams does not commit the fallacy of equivocation. Adrian S. Piper represents the Kantian impartialist's concern that critiques of impartialism equivocate between impartiality and impersonality (Piper, 1987). Consider the example of William Godwin, an early exponent of utilitarianism, who claimed that he would save a benefactor to humanity from a burning building rather than a chambermaid – even if the latter were his mother. Utilitarianism is an impartial view, but is it committed to this kind of cold impersonality? The impartialist says 'no': That objection confuses the impartial versus partial distinction with the personal versus impersonal distinction.

It seems unlikely that Williams committed this elementary error given that he draws attention to it: 'Rawls claims that impartiality does not mean impersonality' – and he does not go on to deny it (Williams, 1981b, p. 5). Williams used the word 'particular' – not 'personal' – positively to characterise his own views in a contrast with the universal. Kantian impartiality, on this understanding, seeks to abstract from the particular to identify principles that are universal. More substantively, Williams believed in basic ('not inferred') reasons of partiality.

As an example of the latter, Williams presented a much-discussed example of an individual who, given the choice between saving one of two people who are at risk of drowning, saves his own wife (Williams, 1981b). Academic commentary has focused on Williams's claim that any impartialist treatment of the case involves 'one thought too many' (Williams, 1981b). This commentary clearly envisages the structure of the problem as whether impartiality can underwrite the claims of the personal.

Williams objects that impartial theories have no business writing back in permissions to be partial to one's 'nearest and dearest'. But the further aspect of his discussion is that the phenomenology of our ethical experience involves basic, partial, reasons. 'That (he or) she is my wife' is a basic reason that does not need to be inferred from any deeper theoretical justification. Williams is committed to the existence of partial reasons in ethics. An initial problem here is that our ordinary word 'partial' equivocates between an ethical idea and a different idea of unfairness, or chauvinism. (John Cottingham calls the latter 'tainted partialism' (Cottingham, 1997)). But that equivocation, once clarified, can be set aside.

For Williams, the fundamental problem with impartialism is its insistence that it represents the claims of morality as both supremely important and rationally authoritative. This, for Williams, renders problematic the relationship between this point of view and others, which also claim 'significance or structural importance in life' (Williams, 1981b, p. 2). For which agents are these concerns important and authoritative: Rational agents as they are or rational agents as they might be if we accept the impartialist's stipulation?

This general thesis underpins the more specific charges that impartialism confines our freedom and alienates us from our ground projects. In his helpful discussion, Paul Hurley notes that the metaphysicians of rightness think they can evade these phenomenological arguments (Hurley, 2009). Moral psychology is not their concern: Modelling the right-making features of actions by explaining the relation between the intrinsic value of outcomes and the nature of rightness is, they think, the only topic in their remit. As Hurley reads Williams – to my mind accurately – this leaves open the relationship between rightness and our ordinary notion of a reason. Therein lies the problem.

This is precisely the gap that we saw Kant close by stipulation: The moral point of view is the supremely important point of view as it reflects our most important values. Its special reasons have rational authority over our other reasons. Throughout this section, we will see Williams asking – once again – why we ought to accept this stipulation. From his perspective, to have an ethical point of view is to be committed to certain ground projects that give substance to the idea of individual character (Williams, 1981b, p. 5). This is not the quest for absolute authenticity in the form of distinctiveness: The content of a ground project can be the same as many other people's projects. What is distinctive is that it is one's own (Williams, 1981b, p. 15). Nevertheless, it is important to Williams that one inhabit a social world in which it matters that we are not all the same. This lack of fungibility is particularly important when it comes to personal relations, including friendship: A person does not want to feel that he or she is simply 'inter-substitutable' (Williams, 1981b, p. 15).

Even if such a project gives each person a reason to go on, this does not make it a selfish project. However, there is still a distinction to be drawn when it comes to the involvement of the self in the success of a project. It can matter to a person that she be the author of its success: That is true even of moral projects. To take Williams's example, ending injustice might be reflected in a person conceding that another person's way of achieving that matters more than her own agency in bringing it about. Yet, a wholly other-regarding aim may still involve the goal of wanting to be the person that brings it about (Williams, 1981b, p. 14).

Ethical impartialism, then, problematises in a general way this relationship between a person and their ground projects. The most famous of Williams's arguments are the two memorable vignettes he presents in 'A Critique of Utilitarianism'. George, a researcher in chemistry, is hampered by ill health from finding work he can do and stays at home to look after his young children. His wife, who holds no strong views about chemical weapons research, works to support the whole family. (So we can presume that she would have no strong principled objections were George to take the job.) This predicament can be eased by George's mentor who can arrange for him to take a well-remunerated job in chemical weapons research. George demurs, at which point his mentor notes that if he does not take the job, a zealot in the cause of chemical weapons research will do so instead.

Jim, a lost and hapless traveller, finds himself in a South American country where the local representatives of a repressive regime – led by the 'sweat stained' Captain Pedro – propose to execute twenty of the indigenous inhabitants to terrorise the local population. Pedro's offer to Jim is that if he kills one of the captives, the other nineteen will be freed. Failing that, all twenty will die.

I will examine these examples in more detail in the next section. At this point, I want simply to note the fundamental issue they raise about a person's relation to their self-conception, their projects, and what they are prepared to 'live with'. These depend, on Williams's view, on a generalisable error: He thinks that the Kantian impartialist misrepresents the relation between a person and her ground projects, but this is a general failing of all forms of impartialism.

The rational authority of impartial morality is such that in any conflict with a ground project it 'must be required to win'. The error here, for Williams, is the absorption of the individual into the moral self in a way that loses the *particularity* of the individual. This is a specific illustration of his more general claim that there are some parts of our ordinary ethical outlook that the impartial perspective must fail to include within its scope:

> Life has to have substance if anything is to have sense, including adherence to the impartial system; but if it has substance, then it cannot grant supreme importance to the impartial system, and that system's hold on it will be, at the limit, insecure. (Williams, 1981b, p. 18)

This is not a denial that there are moral reasons; it expresses the idea that there are moral reasons as the impartialist understands them, but only if there are other reasons, too. This is the asymmetric dependence I have identified between the commitments of the Morality System and those of our ordinary ethical outlook. I will now turn to how this idea plays out in Williams's critique of a specific form of impartial theory: an act utilitarian form of consequentialism.

5.3 Williams's Critique of Consequentialism

George and Jim above are central examples in the literature that has evolved in response to Williams's essay; Williams later expressed some unhappiness, however, with the way he had framed the issue. The most important, methodological, point is that Williams did not take himself to be supplying practical verdicts that differed from those an act utilitarian might give to the two cases. [16] The point is not the verdicts, but the kinds of considerations that supported them. Furthermore, given that he did not share the methodological approach of his opponents, Williams did not think he was in the business of supplying counter-examples to putative principles.

In his work as a whole, Williams showed a great deal of sympathy with the view known as ethical particularism (Thomas, 2011) [17]. This is the claim that ethical thinking can get along perfectly well without being modelled as a finite

---

[16] Thus it is irrelevant that Williams thinks that George ought not to take the job while Jim ought to kill one to save the other nineteen (Williams, 1973b, p. 117; 1995k, pp. 213–215).

[17] This immediately brings out Williams's sympathies for ethical particularism 'moral thought requires abstraction from any particular circumstances and particular characteristics of the parties, including the agent, except in so far as these can be treated as universal features of any morally similar situation' (Williams, 1981b, p. 2)

set of finite principles. He never refined this into a specific objection to principled ethics, perhaps because he thought his critique of the Morality System subsumed it. In the case of his critique of act utilitarianism, however, he protested that he had not invented a counter-example to a principle so as to invite the re-formulation of a refined (and presumably more adequate) principle. Nor, more specifically, did he take himself to have invited the 'integrity objection' to act utilitarianism. I will open the discussion, as Williams did, by highlighting some issues of formulation to identify whether we are discussing a distinctive view here at all.

5.3.1 The Distinctiveness of Act Utilitarianism

It is important, in what follows, to understand what makes act utilitarianism distinctive. As he develops the point, Williams notes that the general account might need adjustment for the concept of central interest to the utilitarian, namely, utility. The first pass at a distinctively consequentialist account of what it is for an agent to act rightly is, for S, where 'S' is 'some concrete particular situation': (Williams, 1973b, p. 97):

(1) In S, he did the right thing in doing A.
     The consequentialist then explains the truth of (1) via the truth of (2):
(2) The state of affairs P is better than any other state of affairs accessible to [the agent].
     This is where Williams first notes that, for the case of utility or well-being, we might have difficulty separating process from product: Things going well for a person (an active state) versus well-being (an end state). If we make an adjustment for these cases it leads to:
(3) The state of affairs which consists in [the agent's] doing A is better than any other state of affairs accessible to [the agent].

Williams thinks that some non-consequentialists will think (1) cannot be explained by (3) because they deny the very idea of all states of affairs being comparable 'from a moral point of view' (Williams, 1973b, p. 88). A version of that very strong 'cannot' is Philippa Foot's view that the idea of the value of an outcome from no person's point of view in particular is a chimera (Foot, 1983).

Williams does not press this point. He notes instead that other non-consequentialists, who do accept the comparability of states of affairs from a putatively moral point of view, nevertheless note the following fact. It could, in general, be true that a state of affairs in which more people kept their promises would be better than a state of affairs in which fewer do. Yet a person might do the right thing by keeping their promise, yet, by that very act, cause fewer people to keep their promises overall. Only if the person acted wrongly (by their own lights) in breaking a promise would more promises be kept overall (Williams, 1973b, pp. 88–89).

The non-consequentialist does not, in terms of the above analysis, think that (3) follows from (1) even if one concedes the comparability of states of affairs. The question is what assumption underpins this demarcation of the non- consequentialist from the consequentialist point of view (given that the latter has relaxed the strict exclusion of action from outcome so as to explain utility itself):

> If the goodness of the world were to consist in people's fulfilling their obligations, it would by no means follow that one of my obligations was to bring it about that other people kept their obligations. (Williams, 1973b, p. 89)

However, the consequentialist *does* think that: Hence the vast increase in the scope of the utilitarian agent's obligations to see that all obligations are kept.

There is a short route from this to the ethical issue of paternalism. This raises the political question, as Williams understands it: 'In whose hands does utilitarian decision lie?' (Williams, 1973b, p. 77). Williams later develops this point into a critique of what he calls 'Government House utilitarianism' in *ELP* (Williams, 1985, pp. 108–110). For now – as this is not a book about political philosophy – I simply note that this argument is important to what has been misunderstood as Williams's 'integrity objection' to act utilitarianism. I turn now to our examples of George and Jim and the first formulation of an objection that does, indeed, mention integrity.

5.3.2 Act Utilitarianism: The Self-Refutation Argument

Throughout his 1973b essay, Williams asks a question which is, by now, familiar from his overall critique of the Morality System and its expression in the works of philosophers: To which assumptions are we entitled by stipulation and for which do we need an argument (Williams, 1973b)? Williams's target, the act utilitarian, assumes without argument that she is entitled to the idea that moral reasons are supremely rationally authoritative. In fact, Williams argues, she lacks that entitlement. All we can assume is this: Agents have ordinary ethical reasons that are, for the most part, not the impartial reasons of the utilitarian. We can also assume that ordinary folk psychology contains the ideas of better or worse reasons for action. How, from these innocuous starting points, do we end up with the counter-intuitive conclusions of the act utilitarian, namely that nearly everything we have reason to do is wrong and we rarely have sufficient reason to do what is right (Hurley, 2009)?

To take a representative example: Peter Singer was so concerned by a famine in Bengal that he wrote one of the most famous papers in moral philosophy 'Famine, Affluence and Morality', (Singer, 1972). From an act utilitarian perspective, Singer argued that every citizen of an affluent society is morally required to donate time and resources to the worst off in other societies until the donor's level of utility matched that of the very next beneficiary she could help.

The usual way to explain this thesis is that Singer demonstrated that, given the state of our world, act utilitarianism is a demanding moral theory. But, as Paul Hurley has pointed out, we ought to generalise the conclusion in a different way (Hurley, 2009). Having read Singer's paper, the reader of this Element ought to turn to the practical task of assisting any person with a lower level of utility. Given the divergence between the living standards of the affluent West and those of other countries, there will be numerous candidates for assistance. The reasons to assist each of them present themselves one at a time; the benefactor must respond to each. What happens to the thought that the benefactor has reasons to live a life of her own?

Conversely, if Singer has correctly identified the nature of right action, each of us needs to explain why we seem to lack sufficient reason to act rightly as we go about our business of, for example, buying our child an inexpensive toy with money that could have been donated to charity. Nearly all of us, nearly all the time, are acting wrongly. Furthermore, we seem curiously unable to summon upon the rational motivation to act rightly. How do we end up with these conclusions? Only because we have overlooked the point that act utilitarianism makes no demands at all, because the idea of a 'demand' attaches to that of an authoritative reason (Hurley, 2006). It is the entitlement to that idea that the act utilitarian needs to demonstrate and not simply assume.

That is not how the act utilitarian sees it: She wants to vindicate the idea that an agent ought always to bring about, via action, the best outcome impartially considered. That is the end point of an argument: The starting point is the data of our ordinary moral experience. Experience tells us that there are reasonably partial reasons. It also seems to tell us that we recognise the values of things from our personal point of view. It also has an intuitive idea of good reasons for action. The act utilitarian wants to deliver a mixed verdict: Some of these assumptions are defensible, but some are not. But as we have seen, Williams claims that, in the process, the view simply helps itself to the idea of the rational authority of moral reasons (Williams, 1973b, 1981b).

Suppose, instead, that the act utilitarian starts her argument by stipulating the truth of this assumption: She makes an announcement that every agent always has most reason to promote the best state of affairs impartially considered.

That simply abandons most of our ordinary ethical commitments. Why would we start from there?

The act utilitarian might say: We are just unpacking the content of some common-sense truisms, such that everyone ought to act for the best. But that phrase has other, less contentious meanings: It can simply mean to act for one's best reasons, which contains no inherent limitation to consequentialist reasons (Hurley, 2017). This stipulation seems uncompelling.

Perhaps realising this fact, the act utilitarian backtracks: hers is a theory, in her re-formulated strategy, not of rational requirement, but of moral requirement. Williams (and Hurley) detect here a characteristic sleight of hand in the formulation of act utilitarian theory. The act utilitarian develops a theory of moral requirements while helping herself to the idea that moral standards are always rationally authoritative over all other reasons.

This is the underlying explanation of why, in Williams's formulation, act utilitarianism cannot describe the relationship between 'a man's projects and his actions' (Williams, 1973b, p. 100). This is because it depends, for its very formulation, on the class of non-impartial reasons that it rejects. The whole view thereby commits the fallacy of equivocation. It gives an account of the content of moral standards such that moral reasons can only be some reasons amongst others. It combines that with the thought that these impartial reasons have ultimate rational authority over all reasons. That is an equivocation in scope. It is why the view is, when thought through, self-undermining: it both presupposes, and undercuts, its own rational authority.

Williams takes as his test case an example on which both he and the act utilitarian ought to be able to agree: utility (Williams, 1973b, p. 80). Intuitively, it seems that if the act utilitarian cannot make sense of happiness, or well-being, that is going to be a serious problem for the view. Well-being, Williams notes, has this complicating feature: For the consequentialist in general, the values of actions 'lie in their causal properties' of producing states of affairs that are the bearers of intrinsic value (Williams, 1973b, p. 84). Yet that seems to make the consequentialist's account of well-being problematic from the outset: People living well, we might say, cannot separate the activity of living well from its value for them. Furthermore, happiness cannot be an agent's direct aim; it supervenes on other things at which the agent directly aims (Williams, 1973b, pp. 110–111).

While accommodating a range of different kinds of projects, Williams insists that utilitarianism must concede the existence of 'commitments' (Williams, 1973b, p. 112). The commitment to being happy is empty; happiness consists in the satisfaction of other commitments to projects that are worthwhile (ibid.). What we now need to do is to plug into the argument the Williams inspired account of an agent's reasons developed above to give us this assumption:

The well-being of an agent is the realisation of various projects, including his or her basic ground project, which grounds all the ends of action that each agent sets him or herself.

Hurley helpfully inserts a missing next step that helps to clarify Williams's earlier argument (it is implicit in what Williams says): You can, of course, think third personally about your projects. By extension, you can do the same for everyone else's projects, too. You could now engage in a new exercise: You could rank outcomes in terms of how many such projects are jointly realised in each outcome in a non-evaluative way. (By ranking here, we must mean merely comparative numerical ranking, not an evaluative ranking.) But, as Hurley notes, there are no reasons in this model. It is all conducted in terms of a proxy for reasons: The third-personal formulation that someone has a reason (where one of those people is, in fact, you). Nothing in this picture contrasts with our common-sense notion of a reason as, at this reflective level, that idea is simply absent.

This impartialist thought experiment began with our ordinary common-sense ethical outlook. That is constituted, for each of us, by our first-personal stand-points that supply the materials for impartial reflection. But in the de-centred view of the Sidgwickian impartialist, this first personality is abstracted away. The first-personal perspective supplies us with reasons for action; the imparti-alist perspective treats these reasons as data. It must presuppose that what I have called its 'reasons proxies' are grounded in actual reasons. But they are not the same thing.

At this crucial point of the argument, Williams notes, you can take this list of different outcomes and create a ranking from it if you are an unusual kind of agent. Let's call this agent 'Jeremy' (in honour of Jeremy Bentham). Jeremy engages in an *optional* ground project with this feature: It is concerned with the realisation of all agents' ground projects. This reflects a feature of act utilitar-ianism Williams noted early in his discussion of the demarcation problem: From its point of view, an act utilitarian agent ought to take an interest not simply in his own obligations, but in the obligations of all other agents.

From the first-personal perspective of this unusual agent, the ranking of outcomes from the third-personal perspective can now be put productively to use. Jeremy takes the third-personal ranking of the joint compossibility of everyone's projects and ranks them evaluatively, in the light of his own ground project, and aligns the judgements in terms of better and worse with his own reasons. *For Jeremy,* his reasons track rightness, which track betterness, in the light of his act utilitarian ground project. He has more reason to bring about those states of affairs that the model ranks as better. Value now enters the picture, as does the connection with rightness. For Jeremy – but only for Jeremy – rightness is now further connected to reasons. Why only for him?

Because Jeremy is impartially benevolent. By introducing this perspective, the third-personal ranking of the compossibility of other people's projects now places each of them on an evaluative scale of better or worse. This correlates with the fact that Jeremy has more or less reason to promote them. This ranking of outcomes is from the moral point of view and he is, in fact, pursuing 'the' moral project (as he would put it). Williams (and Hurley) say: not so fast. As Hurley puts it:

> Consequentialists .... conflate their account of moral standards, properly understood as merely articulating some reasons among others, with an account of such standards as providing ultimate reasons that comprehend all others. (Hurley, 2009, p. 68)

That is, indeed, Williams's diagnosis.

The impartialist conjuring trick is partly the use of the phrase 'higher order' when he or she claims that Jeremy has a higher-order project. That phrase is equivocal: Jeremy, we can all agree, has an unusual ground project in that it takes all other people's ground projects as falling within its scope. But that sense of 'higher order' does not entitle the impartialist to the different sense of the phrase as 'authoritative over'. It does so only if you simply help yourself to the idea that moral reasons are rationally authoritative. But the act utilitarian has no argument at all that entitles her to that assumption. She gave up, recall, on the claim that her view was rationally authoritative for the good reason that it was a very implausible claim.

Instead, she just helps herself to what she needs: Assuming, without argument, that in identifying the 'moral point of view' she has thereby identified the rationally authoritative point of view. But she has not and that helps to explain the peculiarities of the result. She needs to prove a bridging assumption: That the morally required course of action (as she understands that idea) is the rationally, authoritatively, required course of action. But, qua act utilitarian, she has nothing distinctive to say about that claim and no resources to prove it.

Now we can rehearse the same argument again, building in the special features of well-being. A person's well-being, we might say, supervenes on all the projects in her life and it exhibits the feature of transparency. We can 'look through' a good life to the worthwhile projects that constitute it. Take your friend Annika: The good of her life involves her realisation of her projects to be a model professional at work while playing golf excellently qua talented amateur. She acts with the overall aim of living well, but what that means for her differs from the aims of other people.

The first step, for our envisaged act utilitarian agent Jeremy, is to take Annika's project, but not identified as hers, and to combine it with every other agent's projects impartially considered. But from this disengaged perspective there are no reasons. It is only because Jeremy assumes the standpoint of impartial benevolence that we generate evaluative rankings and reasons but that is only for our exceptional agent, Jeremy. By exceptional we do not mean, here, morally exceptional. We mean that the content of his ground project takes as its object the contents of everyone else's ground projects which, as we have seen, are transparent to their objects.

At this point the act utilitarian, such as Jeremy, announces that he has identified the moral point of view. Impartial benevolence *is* the moral project (note the definite article again). It has transformed the third-personal perspective on our ordinary projects into the moral point of view. But now, Williams objects, we run the risk of double counting. Every agent's basic project – which involves all kinds of non-impartial reasons – is supplying the content of Jeremy's 'higher-order' project. But the latter does not encompass or surpass the lower-order projects. It is transparent to them as they are transparent to their objects.

> What projects does the act utilitarian agent have? As a utilitarian, he has the general project of bringing about maximally desirable outcomes ….The desirable outcomes, however, do not just consist of agents carrying out *that* project; there must be other basic or lower-order projects which he and other agents have, and the desirable outcomes are going to consist, in part, of the maximally harmonious realisation of those projects. (Williams, 1973b, p. 110 [Italics in original])

It is just another project, taking its place amongst all the other projects. We can concede that, in terms of scope, Jeremy's unusual ground project encompasses everyone else's project. But it is not a special source of authoritative reasons.

Let's look at the cases of Jeremy and Annika. Jeremy has taken as his ground project the act utilitarian project. We can say this for certain: Jeremy could not be alienated from his ground projects by act utilitarianism because it is his project. So why cannot we simply generalise from Jeremy's case to Annika's case? Because Jeremy's ground project is merely formal: It inherits its content from their non-utilitarian ground projects.

Annika read Peter Singer's paper as an undergraduate and was impressed by it. For her, his project of impartial benevolence is one project amongst their other projects; it generates reasons alongside her other reasons. For her, the impartial perspective is *a* perspective and not *the* perspective. Annika wonders if by playing on public golf courses and not joining an expensive members-only golf club she might have more money to donate to charity. For her, but not for Jeremy, this impartial perspective generates reasons that compete with their other reasons.

Jeremy remonstrates with her: She did not take Singer's lesson to heart. The ground project of impartial benevolence explains what it is for actions to be right. Any other action is wrong. If Annika treats her other, non-impartial, reasons as sufficient reasons for action, then she is acting wrongly. As Hurley points out, what Annika ought to do is take the opposite of Jeremy's advice: To avoid being alienated from her ground projects she should reject act utilitarianism! The introduction of the concept of alienation returns us to Williams's own examples.

Consider George the chemist: Suppose we expand on the example – as Williams invites us to do. Let's expand on George's opposition to chemical weapons by making him a Quaker, who has been mocked by others for his pacifist beliefs and who frequently goes on anti-war demonstrations. Given the constitutive connection that Williams sees between ground projects and reasons, George seems to have very strong reasons not to take the job. Yet George, as a hobby, reads works of moral philosophy and has a further ground project of promoting the projects of all other agents. Now he has two conflicting reasons: His Quaker identity tells him not to take the job while his commitment to utilitarianism tells him to do so. He now asks himself, as Williams puts it, what he is prepared to live with? This is not in his case, as it is third personally, a matter of taking a decision and waiting to see what happens.

George reflects and decides he could not live with himself if he spent his days calculating the effectiveness of precise doses of nerve agents on potential victims. He has a decisive reason not to take the job. His act utilitarian friend – Jeremy once more – phones George to remonstrate with *him*. Jeremy tells George that he has opted for decisive reasons to act wrongly. Action from integrity involves wrongdoing; doing the right involves violating George's integrity from George's point of view. But not from Jeremy's point of view: Were he in George's position, he would be acting rightly, and with integrity, from the compelling and decisive reasons to take the job.

What ought we to conclude? It is tempting to use the characteristic Williams word 'bluff': Jeremy is bluffing. In fact, Jeremy's project has no rational authority over other projects – those without which his project could not exist. We can give George this piece of advice: If he wants to avoid alienation from his fundamental ground project he should not adopt the fundamental ground project of utilitarianism. Indeed, we can say more: If you do not want to live a life where nearly everything you do is wrong, and you can rarely (if at all) find sufficient reason to do right, then do not be an act utilitarian (Hurley, 2009).

Even if this seems plausible it is not clear how integrity is supposed to feature in the example of Jim, invited to execute an innocent person under the coercive pressure of Captain Pedro, who will otherwise execute all twenty. In what sense does that example involve integrity?

5.3.3 Integrity, Revisited

I hope the foregoing makes it clear how unhelpful it is to see Williams's essay as introducing an 'integrity objection' to utilitarianism. This is for several reasons. The first is, as Williams notes in his somewhat rueful account of how his examples have been received, that his point was to ask whether an act utilitarian could make sense of the value of integrity. That is not the same – given the asymmetry between the first person and the third person use of virtue terms that I noted in Section 1 – as the claim that George or Jim should deliberate about what to do using the concept of integrity (Williams, 1981d, p. 49). That does make them both sound morally priggish. Instead, an important aspect of Williams's treatment, particularly in the case of Jim, is that the value of integrity is introduced as 'closely connected' to the idea that 'each of us is specially responsible for what he does, rather than for what other people do' (Williams, 1973b, p. 99).

Going back to the initial demarcation issue: On the one hand, the scope of the act utilitarian's sphere of responsible agency has radically expanded. On the other hand, however, this agent's sphere of agency now also includes the agency of others. And that agency can be hostile.

All of this follows from the breadth of things that consequentialism permits as accessible options for the agent in virtue of the fact that:

> All causal connexions are on the same level . . .. it makes no difference . . ..
> whether the causation of a state of affairs lies through another agent, or not.
> (Williams, 1973b, p. 94)

This is overdetermined both by the evaluative focus of the view being states of affairs and the principle of impartiality (Williams, 1973b, p. 96). Both come together to ground the strong version of the negative responsibility thesis:

> [I]f I am ever responsible for anything, then I must be just as responsible for
> things that I allow or fail to prevent, as I am for things that I . . .. bring about.
> (Williams, 1973b, p. 95)

Both of Williams's cases involve negative responsibility: If George does not take the job, someone more fanatical will and the development of chemical weapons research will be furthered. If Jim does not shoot one, then the captain will shoot all twenty hostages.

It seems plausible that we have two conceptions of causality fused in our common-sense conception: One is the idea of counterfactual dependence while the other is of a causal process (Hall, 2004). If some hooligans' removal of the warning sign in the middle of the night causes a crash two days later, we might think that causal proximity was too remote to invoke a process here. But had they not removed the sign the crash would not have happened.

Williams notes a similar distinction when he notes that, if Jim does not act, he does not make Pedro shoot twenty people. That precisely leaves out the independent agency of the captain in coercing Jim; what is true is that if Jim refrains, then Pedro murders twenty people: 'There is no acceptable way in which [Jim's] refusal makes Pedro shoot' (Williams, 1973b, p. 109). Williams's critique of negative responsibility is not so much, then, its radical extension but the fact that for any individual agent he or she becomes merely a node in a 'satisfaction system':

> The determination to an indefinite degree of my decisions by other people's projects is just another aspect of my unlimited responsibility to act for the best in a causal framework formed to a considerable extent by their projects. (Williams, 1973b, p. 115)

It is integral to the scope of a utilitarian agent's actions that this field of agency is shaped by a social world in which others pursue their projects (Williams, 1973b, p. 115). What one might call the social dimension to Williams's treatment of the value of integrity is a direct conflict between this aspect of act utilitarian agency and the fact that we have 'commitments'. These are 'deep and extensive' involvements and identification – perhaps to the extent that a person has built their life around them (Williams, 1973b, p. 116). It is 'absurd', Williams thinks, that if the act utilitarian structures one's field of action by the projects of others, then given how the numbers pan out you may be asked to sacrifice your own deepest commitments:

> It is absurd to demand of such a man, when the sums come in from the utility network which the projects of others have in part determined, that he should just step aside from his own project and decision and acknowledge the decision which utilitarian calculation requires. It is to alienate him in a real sense from his actions and the source of his actions in his own convictions. It is thus, in the most literal sense, an attack on his integrity. (Williams, 1973b, pp. 116–117)

The aim, once again, is not to change the answers about Williams's cases; rather, 'to provide other ways of thinking about them' (Williams, 1973b, p. 117).

But we can see that Jim, no less than George, has become (in Marx's phrase) a 'plaything of alien forces'. That those forces are other people's agency does not matter at all from the act utilitarian perspective: 'all causal connexions are on the same level'. Jim's and George's commitments are being suffocated and confined by not just other people's projects but 'the' moral project that takes all others in its scope. Perhaps this would not be a problem had the act utilitarian, like the Kantian impartialist, not simply assumed the truth of the claim that moral reasons are supremely rational important when they are, in fact, unable to make good on that claim.

5.4 Williams's Critique of Contractualism

In his discussion of the project of grounding moral reasons on the very idea of practically rational agency we saw, in Section 1, that Williams thought that the project could not be rehabilitated. He did, however, identify it as a task in which several of his peers were engaged. This reflects the widespread intellectual influence of John Rawls – Williams was prepared to concede the impartialism had some potential as a way of modelling justice (Williams, 1985, p. 64). When he turns to the enterprise of ethical theory, however, he does not directly engage with Rawls's views. Instead, he focuses on the moral contractualism developed by Thomas Scanlon.

I think Scanlon's views are foreshadowed when Williams explains his target notion of an ethical theory (Williams, 1985, p. 71):

> An ethical theory is a theoretical account of what ethical thought and practice are, which account either implies a general test for the correctness of basic ethical beliefs and principles or else implies that there cannot be such a test. (Williams, 1985, p. 72)

Williams's inclusion of Scanlon explains the curious part of this definition – the 'negative kind of ethical theory' (ibid.). Scanlon's contractualism, like the Kantian Categorical Imperative which is its ancestor, rules nothing in. It rules candidate conceptions out.

Scanlonian contractualism proceeds as follows: First, we isolate a narrow part of the moral focused solely on interpersonal justification. The next step is to argue that an action is right if it is not wrong. Wrongness is then defined as being impermissible according to a system of principles that survive a distinctive test: That a person would not reject this candidate set of principles as unreasonable were they put forward as 'a basis for informed, unforced, general agreement' (Scanlon, 1998, p. 193).

Contractualism thus directly addresses the issue of intellectual authority: Our goal of living by a set of principles in the light of which we can offer justifications to each is grounded on the deeper value of mutual recognition. Furthermore, being unjustifiable, in Scanlon's sense, is not a property that tracks some independent property of wrongness: It is that in which wrongness consists. Wrongness is derived from the wronging of one person by another such that the former cannot justify her actions to the latter. Our shared reasons are grounded on shared principles underpinned by an evaluative vision of our moral world as a place of mutual recognition of each other's value.

One of the great merits of Scanlon's position is that the narrowness of its scope is flagged up throughout: 'what we owe to each other' maps out a discrete area of ethics and not its full range. It is the conceptual ties between wrongs, wrongings (of one person by another) and interpersonal justification that are its limited focus. Scanlon hopes to avoid circularity by not involving any evaluative commitments when he appeals to reasonableness: Contractualism supplies a negative test applied to sets of principles. It rules some out – but says nothing about how candidate sets are generated in the first place to become candidates for testing. Individual complaints can be brought against candidate sets by appealing to reasonableness. However, that idea presupposes, but does not directly appeal to, the background conception of value that gives the exercise its context and point. There is, overall, value to living with each other on these terms of mutual respect.

Williams notes, in his discussion of the view in *ELP*, that this is not the foundational impartialism he criticised earlier in the book: Contractualism presupposes agents 'assumed to be already interested in reaching agreement' (Williams, 1985, p. 75). Contractualism generally receives a sympathetic treatment in *ELP*. Williams thinks it does offer an answer to the question of how an ethical theory can have intellectual authority. The main focus of his critique is on the special assumptions he thought it needed for it to exercise such authority. I think the contractualist might reasonably complain that Williams does tend to misrepresent contractualism as a convergent theory which aims at agreement. I think it would be more sympathetic to Scanlon's project to take agreement as a given such that we work out its presuppositions. (That goes hand in hand with the avowed narrowness of Scanlon's focus.) Williams assimilates Scanlon's project to Rawls's project which has a different subject matter. That latter case better fits Williams's characterisation of a common project which seeks agreement on fair terms and which uses Rawls's method of reflective equilibrium (Williams, 1985, p. 99). Williams's only comment is that 'the method is appropriate to constructing an ethical theory under these assumptions, but it is very important how strong these assumptions are' (ibid.).

Williams argues that 'the theory' – and now Rawlsian justice and Scanlonian contractualism are not clearly separated – not only starts within the ethical (as the arguments against foundationalism earlier in *ELP* have shown they must). They are 'doubly' in the ethical world: with a method that incorporates substantive commitments combined with what Rawls would call 'realistically utopian' ideals:

> The factual and the ideal are interestingly related in these assumptions. On the one hand, there are assumptions that apply to any society; on the other, there are ideals for a better or more rational society. In between there is a significant, if

not clearly defined, are of conditions that apply to a certain kind of society –
summarily put, a modern society, where that is to a some extent *an ethical
conception and not merely an historical one.* (Williams, 1985, p. 100)

This is the first appearance in the text of *ELP* of an important idea that
characterises Williams's approach to ethics. Ours is a modern society –
a concept that, as we saw in the previous section, discharges several critical
tasks in Williams's work.

In the present context, it seems as if the same doubts Williams has about
Rawls – or 'Rawlsianism', an even vaguer target – reflect back on Scanlon's
view. But it is unclear that they do. Williams moves from the claim that
Rawlsian justice requires explicit discursive principles, to the claim that it
seeks social consensus on contested issues, to the most general claim that 'the
society represents its values in a set of stateable principles' (Williams, 1985,
p. 100). But it seems a stretch to move the expression of conceptions of justice
in a principled form to the claim that all (or most?) of a society's values be
expressed in this way. Williams then argues that it is characteristic of
a pervasively reflective modern society to seek to represent its values expli-
citly as a transparent set of principles. It then seeks to rank them in order of
priority and further reconcile any conflicts via a 'rationalistic decision procedure' that would eventuate in 'an ethical theory in the fullest sense'
(Williams, 1985, p. 101).

Williams originally made a concession to the contractualist enterprise: That
'the contractualist enterprise is coherent' (Williams, 1985, p. 102). But as the
argument proceeds, the concession is steadily withdrawn, and Williams uses as
his interpretative frame Hegel's critique of the putatively abstract and formal
nature of Kant's moral philosophy:

> Hegel admirably criticized the 'abstract' Kantian morality and contrasted it
> with the notion of Sittlichkeit, a concretely determined ethical existence that
> was expressed in the local folkways, a form of life that made particular sense
> to the people living in it. (Williams, 1985, p. 104)

How does Williams's initially sympathetic of contractualism end up at this
point? His claim is that the contractualist formula contains an inner drive to
universalism: That is why the basis of judgements of 'reasonableness' starts to
'thin', as Williams puts it. Contractualism is re-interpreted as aiming at the
very foundationalist perspective that Williams takes himself to have shown to
be impossible.

Yet I think it is an open question whether the analogy with Hegel's ideas is
appropriate here. As Ken Westphal has argued, it is an interpretative mistake to
contrast Kant's 'empty formalism' with Hegel's rich concretisation of ethical

life – that is not what Hegel says. He says that, were it not possible fully to specify the content of Kant's ethics, then it would be empty and formal – but it can be so specified and Hegel shows you how (Westphal, 2005; Thomas, 2015).

By analogy, then, if contractualism denied its dependence on a presupposed ideal of a community of mutual recognition, then it would be empty, formal, and only able to purchase universal appeal at the cost of making its judgements of reasonableness otiose. However some versions of contractualism do not involve that denial (Darwall, 2009). In framing his argument in terms of there being no natural stopping point for the contractualist enterprise it is worth bearing mind that Williams repeatedly notes that slippery slope arguments are invalid.

One might reasonably conclude that Williams has some sympathy with what one might call the minimal core of contractualism on the understanding that this a narrow part of the ethical. It is certainly not committed to the complex presuppositions of the Morality System. One might reasonably complain against contractualism – in a way that Williams does not – that the conceptual connections between wrongs, wrongings, and reasonable complaints do not have to be treated reductively. [18] The idea that it is part of our conception of an ethical system that mature agents within it want to be able to justify their actions to others would seem to be an idea that Williams endorses – if that claim is understood in a sufficiently minimal way.

Of all of Williams's discussions, then, his critique of contractualism is the most inconclusive. That said, there are multiple routes to the same destination in Williams's work. From everything that he says, we might conclude that contractualism is simply irrelevant, because the phenomenology of our moral experience shows us that ethical reasons are fundamentally partial. Another direct path to that conclusion would be to develop, in a positive way, the kind of particularist view of ethical judgment that argues that it need not be principled and, in fact, it is not (Dancy, 2004; Thomas, 2011). An indirect path would be to argue that Williams's internal reasons thesis about the nature of reasons rules out contractualism. I noted that Williams and Nagel agree about motivated desire theory and the fact that any account of the rationalisation of ethical action had to mention a desire. Scanlon is more drawn to a purely cognitivist view where believing that one has a reason suffices for an agent to act from reasons (Scanlon, 2014).

It is worth recalling at this point Williams's surprising recruitment of Kant to the ranks of internal reasons theorists. While Williams may have his doubts

---

[18] Scanlon can argue that noting an asymmetric dependence between values and reasons is a conceptual claim that need not be viewed as a reduction of the former to the latter. That issue remains open.

about Kant's founding stipulation, as John Skorupski notes there is a concern that Kant and the internal reasons theorist undoubtedly share:

> [M]oral agents are accountable in so far as responsible – able to respond for themselves to moral considerations as a matter of self-governance, not external command. (Skorupski, 2007, p. 74)

It seems, then, that there is a minimal core commitment that Williams and the contractualist share. It seems that if contractualism represents one form of the pathology of theory, whose cultural dominance reflects underlying truths about the prominence of the Morality System, or the social pressures of modernity, then it is on the field of those wider engagements that Williams's conflict with contractualism ought to be fought.

5.5 What Can a Person Live With?

As I have previously noted, Williams was influenced by Winch's 'The Universalisability of Moral Judgement' (Winch, 1965). In this section, we have concluded that moral philosophy, in the form of theory, gives us no 'tests' in either its positive or negative variants. But we are left with this question, which Williams poses more than once, and which seems to take its cue from Winch: What can a person live with?

Is that our substitute for a 'test' when we think reflectively about the ethical? In Winch's discussion, Vere thought he could live with condemning Budd to death: He was doubly wrong both in his verdict on Budd and about himself. When our ethical dispositions are focused on an ethical question we face a dual task: of looking outwards, to the demands of the case, and inwards – to what we know about ourselves. George the potential chemical weapons researcher and Jim, the potentially coerced killer of an innocent victim both have to ask themselves: What can I live with? Charles Taylor notes that these questions pose a special challenge:

> [O]ur evaluations are more open to challenge precisely in virtue of the very character of depth which we see in the self. For it is precisely the deepest evaluations which are least clear, least articulated, most easily subject to illusion and distortion. (Taylor, 1976, pp. 296–297)

Williams envisages a continuity between everyday ethical decisions and these radical choices where our most fundamental identifications are challenged in this kind of disorienting way. Through ethical decision, we find out who we are, or shape who we are, in ways that can be mistaken – disastrously so for Vere. In his culminating discussion, in *Truth and Truthfulness*, Williams notes that we can describe this task in general terms (Williams, pp. 191–205) But these observations are no substitute for reflective decision.

This late discussion is helpful in several ways: First, Williams remained committed to the idea that reasoning *from* one's must fundamental identifications marks off some of our most important ethical deliberations. This is so even if, as Taylor implies, such decisions are dizzying at altitude: These questions about who we are and aspire to be leave behind the familiar criteria of more mundane decisions. Again, concerned to address the charge of unwarranted egotism, Williams argues that we seek to act in the light of identifications that others can acknowledge. And we are persistently hampered, in taking such decisions, by the ease with which belief can be suborned by fantasy and wish (Williams, 2002, p. 197). Self-deception is an obstacle both to taking the correct ethical decision and, in the process, knowing who we are. Here, too, other people play a role as a resource for the 'steadying' of our minds (ibid.). We can begin to appreciate why Williams thought that the resources of academic moral philosophy were not of much help in answering questions of this kind.

Abbreviations of Book Titles

Problems of the Self	*PS*
Moral Luck	*ML*
Ethics and the Limits of Philosophy	*ELP*
Making Sense of Humanity	*MSH*
Shame and Necessity	*S&N*
Truth and Truthfulness	*T&T*

References

I. Books by Williams

Morality: An Introduction to Ethics (Cambridge University Press, 1972).

(1973a) *Problems of the Self: Philosophical Papers 1956–197* (Cambridge University Press, 1973a).

(1973b) *Utilitarianism: For and Against*, (by J. J. C. Smart and Bernard Williams) (Cambridge University Press, 1973b).

Descartes: The Project of Pure Enquiry (Penguin, 1978).

Moral Luck: Philosophical Papers 1973–1980 (Cambridge University Press, 1981).

Ethics and the Limits of Philosophy (Routledge, 1985).

Shame and Necessity (California University Press, 1993).

Making Sense of Humanity, and Other Philosophical Papers 1982–1993 (Cambridge University Press, 1995).

Plato: The Invention of Philosophy (Phoenix, 1998).

Truth and Truthfulness (Princeton University Press, 2002).

In the Beginning Was the Deed: Realism and Moralism in Political Argument (Princeton University Press, 2005).

Philosophy as a Humanistic Discipline, edited by A. W. Moore (Princeton University Press, 2006).

The Sense of the Past: Essays in the History of Philosophy, edited by Myles Burnyeat (Princeton University Press, 2009).

Essays and Reviews, 1959–2002 (Princeton University Press, 2014).

II. Papers by Williams

(1981a) 'Preface', *Moral Luck*, pp.ix–xi.

(1981b) 'Persons, Character and Morality', *ML*, pp.1–19.

(1981c) 'Moral Luck', *ML*, pp.20–39.

(1981d) 'Utilitarianism and Moral Self-Indulgence', *ML*, pp.40–53.

(1981e) 'Internal and External Reasons', *ML*, pp.101–113.

(1981f) 'Practical Necessity', ML, pp.124–131.

(1988) 'The Structure of Hare's Theory', in Seanor, Douglas and Fotion, N. (eds.) *Hare and Critics: Essays on Moral Thinking*, Clarendon Press, pp.76–85.

(1995a) 'How Free Does the Will Need to Be?', *Making Sense of Humanity*, pp.3–21.

(1995b) 'Voluntary Act and Responsible Agents', *Making Sense of Humanity*, pp.22–34.

(1995c) 'Internal Reasons and the Obscurity of Blame', *Making Sense of Humanity*, pp.35–45.

(1995d) 'Moral Incapacity', *MSH*, pp.46–55.

(1995e) 'Acts and Omissions, Doing and Not Doing', *Making Sense of Humanity*, pp.56–64.

(1995f) 'Nietzsche's Minimalist Moral Psychology', *Making Sense of Humanity*, pp.65–76.

(1995g) 'The Point of View of the Universe: Sidgwick and the Ambitions of Ethics', *Making Sense of Humanity*, pp.153–171.

(1995h) 'Who Needs Ethical Knowledge?', *Making Sense of Humanity*, pp.203–212.

(1995i) 'Truth in Ethics', *Ratio*, vol. 3, issue 8, pp. 227–242.

(1995j) 'Moral Luck: A Postscript', *Making Sense of Humanity*, pp.241–247.

(1995k) 'Replies' in Altham, J. E. J. and Harrison, T. R. (eds.) *World, Mind and Ethics: Essays on the Ethical Philosophy of Bernard Williams*, Cambridge University Press, pp.185–224.

(2016) 'The Need to be Sceptical' in *Essays and Reviews: 1959–2002*, Princeton University Press, pp.311–318.

III. Other Works Cited

Altham, J. E. J. and Harrison, T. R. (eds.) (1995) *World, Mind and Ethics: Essays on the Ethical Philosophy of Bernard Williams*, Cambridge University Press.

Anscombe, G. E. M. (1958) 'Modern Moral Philosophy', *Philosophy*, vol.33, no.124, pp.1–19.

Bales, Eugene (1971) 'Act Utilitarianism: Account of Right-Making Characteristics or Decision Making Procedure?', *American Philosophical Quarterly*, vol.8, no.3, pp.257–265.

Cottingham, John (1997) 'The Ethical Credentials of Partiality', *Proceedings of the Aristotelian Society*, pp.1–21.

Dancy, Jonathan (2004) *Ethics without Principles*, Oxford University Press.

Darwall, Stephen (2009) *The Second-Person Standpoint: Morality, Respect and Accountability*, Harvard University Press.

Finlay, Stephen (2009) 'The Obscurity of Internal Reasons', *Philosophers Imprint*, vol.9, no.7, pp.1–22.

Foot, Philippa (1978) 'Are Moral Considerations Overriding?', reprinted in *Virtues and Vices*, Blackwell, pp.181–189.

Foot, Philippa (1983) 'Utilitarianism and the Virtues', *Proceedings and Addresses of the APA*, vol.57, no.2, pp.273–283.

Fricker, Miranda (2000) 'Confidence and Irony' in Edward Harcourt (ed.) *Morality, Reflection and Ideology*, Oxford University Press, pp.87–112.

Hall, Ned (2004) 'Two Concepts of Causation', in John Collins, Ned Hall, and Laurie Paul (eds.) *Causation and Counterfactuals*, MIT Press, pp.225–276.

Hare, R. M. (1981) *Moral Thinking: Its Levels, Method, and Point*, Oxford University Press.

Hornsby, Jennifer (2008) 'A Disjunctive Conception of Acting for Reasons', in Adrian Haddock and Fiona Macpherson (eds.) *Disjunctivism: Perception, Action, Knowledge*, Oxford University Press, pp.244–261.

Hurley, Paul (2006) 'Does Consequentialism Make Too Many Demands, or None at All?', *Ethics*, vol.116, no.4, pp.680–706.

Hurley, Paul (2009) *Beyond Consequentialism*, Oxford University Press.

Hurley, Paul (2017) 'Why Consequentialism's Compelling Idea Is Not', *Social Theory and Practice*, vol.43, no.1, pp.29–54.

Kagan, Shelley (1989) *The Limits of Morality*, Oxford University Press.

Larmore, Charles (2010) *Practices of the Self*, Chicago University Press.

Macintyre, Alasdair (1981) *After Virtue: A Study in Moral Theory*, Duckworth.

MacIntyre, Alasdair (2016) *Ethics in the Conflicts of Modernity: An Essay on Desire, Practical Reasoning and Narrative*, Cambridge University Press.

McDowell, John (1985) 'Values and Secondary Qualities' in Ted Honderich (ed.) *Morality and Objectivity*, Routledge, pp.110–129.

Mill, John Stuart (1861/1998) 'Of the Ultimate Sanction of the Principle of Utility' in Roger Crisp (ed.) *Utilitarianism*, Oxford University Press, pp. 27–34.

Moore, A. W. (2007) 'Realism and the Absolute Conception' in Thomas, Alan (ed.) *Bernard Williams*, pp.24–46.

Moore, A. W. (2003) 'Williams on Ethics, Knowledge and Reflection', *Philosophy*, vol.78, no.305, pp. 337–354.

Nagel, Thomas (1970) *The Possibility of Altruism*, Oxford University Press.

Nagel, Thomas (1986) *The View from Nowhere*, Oxford University Press.

Nagel, Thomas (1991) *Equality and Partiality*, Oxford University Press.

Nagel, Thomas (1997) *The Last Word*, Oxford University Press.

Nussbaum, Martha (1995) 'Aristotle on Human Nature and the Foundations of Ethics', in Altham, J. E. J. and Harrison, T. R. (eds.) pp.86–131.

Parfit, Derek (1984) *Reasons and Persons*, Oxford University Press.

Piper, Adrian S. (1987) 'Moral Theory and Moral Alienation', *Journal of Philosophy*, vol.84, no.2, pp.102–118.

Rawls, John (1971/1999) *A Theory of Justice*, Belknap Press.

Sacks, Mark (2005) 'Sartre, Strawson and Others', *Inquiry*, vol.48, no.3, pp.275–299.

Sartre, Jean-Paul (1956) *Being and Nothingness*, trans. Hazel Barnes, Washington Square Books.

Scanlon, Thomas (1998) *What We Owe to Each Other*, Harvard University Press.

Scanlon, Thomas (2014) *Being Realistic about Reasons*, Oxford University Press.

Scheffler, Samuel (1982) *The Rejection of Consequentialism*, Oxford University Press.

Sidgwick, Henry (1907/1962) *The Methods of Ethics*, Hackett Classics.

Singer, Peter (1972) 'Famine, Affluence and Morality', *Philosophy & Public Affairs*, vol. 1, no. 3, pp. 229–243.

Skorupski, John (2007) 'Internal Reasons and the Scope of Blame', in Thomas, Alan (ed), Bernard Williams, pp. 73–103.

Stevens, Wallace (1954) *The Collected Poems*, Alfred A. Knopf.

Strawson, Peter F. (1971) 'Meaning and Truth', in Logic-Linguistic Papers, Methuen, pp. 170–189.

Stroud, Barry (2011) 'Practical Reasoning' in *Philosophers Past and Present*, Oxford University Press, pp.207–222.

Taylor, Charles (1976) 'Responsibility for Self' in Amelie Rorty (ed.) *The Identities of Persons*, University of California Press, pp. 281–299.

Taylor, Charles (1989) *Sources of the Self*, Harvard University Press.

Thomas, Alan (2002) 'Internal Reasons and Contractualist Impartiality', *Utilitas*, vol.14, no.2, pp.135–154.

Thomas, Alan (2005) 'Reasonable Partiality and the Agent's Personal Point of View', *Ethical Theory and Moral Practice*, vol. 8, no. 1/2, pp. 25–43.

Thomas, Alan (2006) *Value and Context: The Nature of Moral and Political Knowledge*, Clarendon Press.

Thomas, Alan (ed.) (2007) *Bernard Williams: Contemporary Philosophy in Focus*, Cambridge University Press.

Thomas, Alan (2009) *Thomas Nagel*, Acumen Press.

Thomas, Alan (2010) 'Alienation, Objectivity and the Primacy of Virtue' in Jonathan Webber (ed.) *Reading Sartre*, Routledge, pp.161–179.

Thomas, Alan (2011) 'Another Particularism: Reasons, Status and Defaults', *Ethical Theory and Moral Practice*, vol.14, no.2, pp.151–167.

Thomas, Alan (2015) 'Integrity, Ground Projects and Reasons to Be Moral', in Beatrix Himmelmann and Robert Louden (eds.) *Why Be Moral?* De Gruyter, pp.249–271.

Thomas, Alan (2017) 'Rawls and Political Realism', *European Journal of Political Theory*, vol.16, no.3, pp.304–324.

Thomas, Alan (2019) 'Does Epistemic Injustice Involve "Corrective Virtue"?' in Mark LeBar (ed.) *Becoming Virtuous: Justice*, Oxford University Press, pp.209–236.

Thomas, Alan (2024) 'Virtue, Authenticity and Irony: Themes from Sartre and Williams', *Topoi*. URL: https://doi.org/10.1007/s11245-023-09985-4

Westphal, Kenneth (2005) 'Kant, Hegel and Determining Our Duties', *Annual Review of Law and Ethics*, no.13, pp.335–354.

Wiggins, David (2000) *Needs, Values, Truth*, 3rd edition, Blackwells.

Winch, Peter (1965) 'The Universalisability of Moral Judgement', *The Monist*, vol.49, no.2, pp.196–214.

Wright, Crispin (1992) *Truth and Objectivity*, Harvard University Press.

Acknowledgements

I was fortunate to be taught by Bernard Williams. He was a teacher, mentor, and friend whom I remember with great affection. That was an advantage for writing a book of this kind. Equally, it was an advantage to be taught by those with a deep understanding of his work: Ross Harrison, Naomi Eilan, the late Mark Sacks and, above all, Adrian Moore.

Limitations of scope have made it practically impossible to engage with the emerging literature on Williams's work. I was forced to be selective, but my views have undoubtedly been shaped by friends and colleagues such as Edward Harcourt, Miranda Fricker, Paul Hurley, and David Owen. David offered insightful comments on the whole manuscript. So did the dedicatee of this Element, Kathryn Brown, to whom I wish to dedicate this book. I am, as always, immensely grateful for her wise counsel.

Cambridge Elements ⁼

Ethics

Elements in the Series

A full series listing is available at: www.cambridge.org/EETH

9 781108 706421